ANGELS

In this tremendously reassuring and inspiring best seller, the world's most famous clergyman says:

"The empire of angels is as vast as God's creation. If you believe the Bible, you will believe in their ministry. They crisscross the Old and New Testaments, being mentioned directly or indirectly nearly three hundred times.

"In the midst of the world crisis through which we are destined to live in the years ahead, the subject of angels will be of great comfort and inspiration to believers in God—and a challenge to unbelievers to believe.

"The Scripture says there is a time to be born and a time to die. And when my time to die comes, an angel will be there to comfort me. He will give me peace and joy even at that most critical hour, and usher me into the presence of God, and I will dwell with the Lord forever. Thank God for the ministry of His blessed angels!"

Books by Billy Graham

Angels: God's Secret Agents
My Answer
Peace with God
The Secret of Happiness!
World Aflame

Published by POCKET BOOKS

ANGELS:
God's Secret Agents

BILLY GRAHAM

world wide publications
1303 Hennepin Avenue • Minneapolis, Minnesota 55403

ANGELS: GOD'S SECRET AGENTS

Doubleday edition published 1975

POCKET BOOK edition published April, 1977

This POCKET BOOK edition includes every word contained in the original, higher-priced edition. It is printed from brand-new plates made from completely reset, clear, easy-to-read type.
POCKET BOOK editions are published by
POCKET BOOKS,
a division of Simon & Schuster, Inc.,
A GULF+WESTERN COMPANY
630 Fifth Avenue,
New York, N.Y. 10020.
Trademarks registered in the United States
and other countries.

Contents

Contents

Preface

When I decided to preach a sermon on angels, I found practically nothing in my library. Upon investigation I soon discovered that little had been written on the subject in this century. This seemed a strange and ominous omission. Bookstores and libraries have shelves of books on demons, the occult and the devil. Why was the devil getting so much more attention from writers than angels? Some people seem to put the devil on a par with God. Actually, Satan is a fallen angel.

Burne-Jones wrote to Oscar Wilde that "the more materialistic science becomes, the more angels shall I paint: their wings are my protest in favor of the immortality of the soul."

John Calvin in Volume 1 of his *Institutes of the Christian Religion* said, "Angels are the dispensers and administrators of the divine beneficence toward us. They regard our safety, undertake our defense, direct our ways, and exercise a constant solicitude that no evil befall us."

Angels have a much more important place in the Bible than the devil and his demons. Therefore, I undertook a biblical study of the subject of angels. Not only has it been one of the most fascinating studies of my life, but I believe the subject is more relevant today than perhaps at any time in history.

The Bible teaches that angels intervene in the affairs of nations. God often uses them to execute judgment on nations. They guide, comfort and provide for the people of God in the midst of suffering and persecution. Martin Luther once said in *Tabletalk*, "An angel is a spiritual creature without a body created by God for the service of christendom and the church."

In the midst of the world crisis through which we are destined to live in the years ahead, the subject of angels will be of great comfort and inspiration to believers in God—and a challenge to unbelievers to believe.

Pascal once said, "Certain authors, when they speak of their work, say 'my book,' 'my commentary,' 'my history.' They would be better to say 'our book,' 'our commentary,' 'our history,' since their writings generally contain more of other peoples' good things than their own."

This is our book, and I wish to thank all who have helped me with this intriguing and sometimes complicated subject.

In its writing, editing and counseling, I am

indebted to—Ralph Williams, who helped with research for my original writing of the manuscript; Dr. Harold Lindsell, editor of *Christianity Today*, who went through the original manuscript with many helpful suggestions; to Mr. Paul Fromer, professor at Wheaton College, who helped with content, style and organization.

To my faithful staff at Montreat who typed, retyped, read and called to my attention many areas of possible improvement—Karlene Aceto, Elsie Brookshire, Lucille Lytle, Stephanie Wills and Sally Wilson.

To Calvin Thielman, Pastor of Montreat Presbyterian Church; and Dr. John Akers, Dean of Montreat-Anderson College, for their suggestions.

To Ruth, who was an encouragement and a help from start to finish while recuperating from a serious accident.

Especially, to our heavenly Father who helped me see this neglected and important subject.

Through the months I have gathered ideas and even quotations from sources long-since forgotten. To everyone whose books and articles I have read, to every man or woman with whom I have talked or prayed about the subject of angels, I express my gratitude. Each has contributed to this book. I regret it is not possible to list each one by name.

It is my prayer that God will use this book to bring comfort to the sick and the dying; to bring encouragement to those who are under the pressures of everyday living; to bring guidance to those who are frustrated by the events of our generation.

Billy Graham

Montreat, North Carolina
October 1, 1975

ANGELS:
God's Secret Agents

CHAPTER 1

Why This Book on Angels?

My wife, who was born and raised in China, recalls that in her childhood days tigers lived in the mountains. One day a poor woman went up to the foothills to cut grass. To her back was tied a baby, and a little child walked beside her. In her hand she carried a sharp sickle to cut grass. Just as she reached the top of a hill she heard a roar. Frightened almost speechless she looked around to see a mother tigress springing at her, followed by two cubs. This illiterate Chinese mother had never attended school or entered a church. She had never seen a Bible. But a year or two earlier a missionary had told her about Jesus, "who is able to help you when you are in trouble." As the claws of the tigress tore her arm and shoulder, the woman cried out in a frenzy, "Oh Jesus, help me!" This ferocious beast, instead of attacking again to get an easy meal, suddenly turned and ran away.

The Bible says, "He will give his angels charge

of you, to guard you in all your ways" (Psalm 91:11 RSV). Had God sent an angel to help this poor ignorant Chinese woman? Are there supernatural beings today who are able to influence the affairs of men and nations?

Help from Angels

Dr. S. W. Mitchell, a celebrated Philadelphia neurologist, had gone to bed after an exceptionally tiring day. Suddenly he was awakened by someone knocking on his door. Opening it he found a little girl, poorly dressed and deeply upset. She told him her mother was very sick and asked him if he would please come with her. It was a bitterly cold, snowy night, but though he was bone tired, Dr. Mitchell dressed and followed the girl.

As *Reader's Digest* reports the story, he found the mother desperately ill with pneumonia. After arranging for medical care, he complimented the sick woman on the intelligence and persistence of her little daughter. The woman looked at him strangely and then said, "My daughter died a month ago." She added, "Her shoes and coat are in the clothes closet there." Dr. Mitchell, amazed and perplexed, went to the closet and opened the door. There hung the very coat worn by the little girl who had brought him to tend to her mother. It was warm and dry and could not possibly have been out in the wintry night.

Could the doctor have been called in the hour of

14

desperate need by an angel who appeared as this woman's young daughter? Was this the work of God's angels on behalf of the sick woman?

The Reverend John G. Paton, a missionary in the New Hebrides Islands, tells a thrilling story involving the protective care of angels. Hostile natives surrounded his mission headquarters one night, intent on burning the Patons out and killing them. John Paton and his wife prayed all during that terror-filled night that God would deliver them. When daylight came they were amazed to see the attackers unaccountably leave. They thanked God for delivering them.

A year later, the chief of the tribe was converted to Jesus Christ, and Mr. Paton, remembering what had happened, asked the chief what had kept him and his men from burning down the house and killing them. The chief replied in surprise, "Who were all those men you had with you there?" The missionary answered, "There were no men there; just my wife and I." The chief argued that they had seen many men standing guard—hundreds of big men in shining garments with drawn swords in their hands. They seemed to circle the mission station so that the natives were afraid to attack. Only then did Mr. Paton realize that God had sent His angels to protect them. The chief agreed that there was no other explanation. Could it be that God had sent a legion of angels to protect His servants, whose lives were being endangered?

A Persian colporteur was accosted by a man who asked him if he had a right to sell Bibles.

"Why, yes," he answered, "we are allowed to sell these books anywhere in the country!" The man looked puzzled, and asked, "How is it, then, that you are always surrounded by soldiers? I planned three times to attack you, and each time, seeing the soldiers, I left you alone. Now I no longer want to harm you." Were these soldiers heavenly beings?

During World War II, Captain Eddie Rickenbacker was shot down over the Pacific Ocean. For weeks nothing was heard of him. The newspapers reported his disappearance and across the country thousands of people prayed. Mayor LaGuardia asked the whole city of New York to pray for him. Then he returned. The Sunday papers headlined the news, and in an article, Captain Rickenbacker himself told what had happened. "And this part I would hesitate to tell," he wrote, "except that there were six witnesses who saw it with me. A gull came out of nowhere, and lighted on my head —I reached up my hand very gently—I killed him and then we divided him equally among us. We ate every bit, even the little bones. Nothing ever tasted so good." This gull saved the lives of Rickenbacker and his companions. Years later I asked him to tell me the story personally, because it was through this experience that he came to know Christ. He said, "I have no explanation except that God sent one of His angels to rescue us."

During my ministry I have heard or read literally thousands of similar stories. Could it be that these were all hallucinations or accidents or fate or luck? Or were real angels sent from God to perform certain tasks?

The Current Cult of the Demonic

Just a few years ago such ideas would have been scorned by most educated people. Science was king, and science was tuned in to believe only what could be seen or measured. The idea of supernatural beings was thought to be nonsense, the ravings of the lunatic fringe.

All this has changed. Think, for example, of the morbid fascination modern society has for the occult.

Walk into a book store in London; visit any newsstand at a modern airport; go to a university library. You will be confronted by shelves and tables packed with books about the devil, Satan worship and demon possession. A number of Hollywood films, television programs and as many as one in four hard-rock pop songs are devoted to, or thematically make reference to, the devil. The Rolling Stones sang their "Sympathy for the Devil" to the top of the popularity chart; another group answered back with a symphony to the devil.

The Exorcist has already proved to be one of the biggest money-makers of any film in history. Arthur Lyons gave his book a title that is frighteningly accurate: *The Second Coming: Satanism in America.* This theme, which intellectuals would have derided a generation ago, is now being dealt with seriously by university professors such as John Updike and Harvey Cox. Some polls indicate that 70 per cent of Americans believe in a personal devil. Walter Cronkite announced a poll over CBS network news showing that the number of Americans who now believe in a personal devil has increased 12 per cent. It is ironic that a generation ago, scientists, psychologists, sociologists and even some theologians were predicting that by the late 1970s there would be a sharp decline in the belief in the supernatural. The reverse is true!

Some time ago, in a medium-sized metropolitan area, I turned out of curiosity to the entertainment pages of the local newspaper and studied them carefully. I was unprepared for the shock I received as I read the descriptions of the themes and content of the feature motion pictures being shown in the theaters in that area. They focused on sadism, murder, demon possession and demonism, devil worship and horror, not to mention those that depicted erotic sex. It seemed that each advertisement tried to outdo the others in the degree of shock, horror and mind-bending emotional devastation.

Even in the Christian world the presses have turned out a rash of books on the devil by both Catholic and Protestant writers. I personally believe we have more than given the devil his due with too many books about him. I tend to think the devil is getting too much attention. Even I wrote a book on the devil and his demons, but have not published it yet. I still am wondering whether I should.

The Reality and Power of Satan

The Bible does teach that Satan is a real being who is at work in the world together with his emissaries, the demons. In the New Testament they intensified their activities and bent every effort to defeat the work of Jesus Christ, God's Son. The apparent increase in satanic activity against people on this planet today may indicate that the Second Coming of Jesus Christ is close at hand. Certainly, the activity of Satan is evident on every side. We can see it in the wars and other crises that affect all men daily. We can also see it in the attacks of Satan against individual members of the body of Christ.

The eminent British surgeon/psychiatrist, Dr. Kenneth McAll, is an authority on the subject of satanology. He spent many years in China, but was forced to return to England, where he took up psychiatry. When he became convinced that hundreds of his patients would not be helped by his surgeon's scalpel or his psychiatrist's couch, he remembered the demonism he had observed firsthand in China in the 1930s. He joined a special task force set up by a top-ranking English clergyman, the late Bishop of Exeter, and is today an international figure who acts as a liaison between the medical profession, the International Fraternity of Psychiatrists, and the Church on matters having to do with satanism, demon possession and exorcism.

Dr. McAll is convinced that ostensibly innocent pastimes such as fortune telling, Ouija boards, tarot cards, white magic, seance experiments and astrology are but the thin edge of the wedge into the realm of Satanism, and should be studiously avoided by children and adults alike. Recently I had dinner with several senators and congressmen in a dining room in the Capitol building. We began discussing the rising interest in the occult with special reference to *The Exorcist.* One of the senators, who had recently passed through a deep religious experience, said that due to his past experience with the occult, whenever he knew of a theater that was showing *The Exorcist* he would drive a block around it. He was afraid even to go near it. He said, "I know that both angels and demons are for real."

Dr. McAll warns that people naively suppose that the recent craze for the occult is a fascinating fad or a passing game. He insists that there are now hundreds of documented cases of individuals who began by dabbling in these things innocently and who ended by being either partially controlled or totally possessed by Satan and his demonic host.

Several years ago Pope Paul said he was sure that the evil forces attacking every level of society had behind them the work of a personal devil with a whole kingdom of demons at his command. The

Roman Catholic Church has been rethinking its position on the reality of the spirit world; and interest in this subject has revived among both theological liberals and evangelicals in Protestant churches everywhere.

Unidentified Flying Objects

The renewed interest in the occult and satanism is not the only evidence of the new openness to the supernatural. It also shows in the widespread revival of speculation about the so-called "unidentified flying objects"—UFOs.

Some reputable scientists deny and others assert that UFOs do appear to people from time to time. Some scientists have reached the place where they think they can prove that these are possibly visitors from outer space. Some Christian writers have speculated that UFOs could very well be a part of God's angelic host who preside over the physical affairs of universal creation. While we cannot assert such a view with certainty, many people are now seeking some type of supernatural explanation for these phenomena. Nothing can hide the fact, however, that these unexplained events are occurring with greater frequency around the entire world and in unexpected places.

Japan recently witnessed a typical example of unexplained objects that appeared in the night skies. On January 15, 1975, a squadron of UFO-like objects, resembling a celestial string of pearls, soared silently through the evening skies over half the length of Japan. As government officials, police and thousands of curious citizens stared at the sky in wonder, from fifteen to twenty glowing objects, cruising in straight formation, flew over Japan inside a strange misty cloud. Further, they were sighted and reported in cities seven hundred miles apart in less than an hour.

Hundreds of frantic telephone calls jammed switchboards of police stations and government installations as the spectacular formation sped south. "All the callers reported seeing a huge cloud passing over the city. They said they saw strange objects inside the cloud moving in a straight line," recalled Duty Officer Takeo Ohira. Were they planes? "No," said Hiroshi Mayazawa, "because no planes or natural phenomena appeared on my radar. It was an exceptionally clear night. To me the whole thing is a mystery."

Professor Masatoshi Kitamura watched the dazzling display in the night sky from the Control Room of Tokyo's Meteorological Bureau station near the airport. He said, "I was mystified. Nothing showed up on my radar. I reported my sighting to the airport control tower and they told me nothing showed on their radar either."

Hundreds of similar events are being reported every year on every continent. A scientist at the atomic laboratory research installation at Los Alamos told me that for every one in twenty of these UFOs that have been investigated no scientific explanation exists. The highly imaginative and speculative theories of some men simply will not do.

Other Explanations

An almost unbelievable rise of interest has occurred in books and films centering in the ideas of Immanuel Velikovsky and Erich von Däniken. Von Däniken in his best seller, *Chariots of the Gods?*, theorizes that in pre-history astronauts from distant stars visited earth in spaceships. From these visits grew man's idea of gods and many of his conceptions of them. Velikovsky in his equally popular *Worlds in Collision* and *Ages in Chaos* puts forward the notion that the turbulent history of the Middle East in the second millennium B.C. can be traced to a violent scattering of the solar system that caused ruin on earth. The knowledge of the intense suffering of those times was soon repressed, but lies buried in man's racial memory, explaining his modern self-destructive behavior.

Men would dismiss these grandiose cosmologies lightly if it were not that they, along with a number of other theories, have been put forward with such frequency and serious import that no one can shrug them off. They are being studied seriously at many of our universities. As a theme for talk shows, hardly anything or anyone can top people like von Däniken and Velikovsky.

Some sincere Christians, whose views are anchored in a strong commitment to Scripture, contend that these UFOs are angels. But are they? These people point to certain passages in Isaiah, Ezekiel, Zechariah and the book of Revelation, and draw parallels to the reports of observers of alleged UFO appearances. They take the detailed descriptions, for example, of a highly credible airline crew and lay them alongside Ezekiel 10, and put forward a strong case. In Ezekiel 10 we read, "Each of the four cherubim had a wheel beside him—'The Whirl-Wheels,' as I heard them called, for each one had a second wheel crosswise within, sparkled like chrysolite, giving off a greenish-yellow glow. Because of the construction of these wheels, the cherubim could go straight forward in each of four directions; they did not turn when they changed direction but could go in any of the four ways their faces looked. . . . and when they rose into the air the wheels rose with them, and stayed beside them as they flew. When the cherubim stood still, so did the wheels, for the spirit of the cherubim was in the wheels" (Ezekiel 10:9–13, 16–17 Living Bible).

Any attempt to connect such passages with the visits of angels may, at best, be speculation. What is interesting, however, is that such theories are now being given serious attention even by people who make no claim to believe in the God of the Bible.

A further evidence of the renewed interest in

the supernatural is the widespread fascination with extrasensory perception—ESP. The subjective science of parapsychology is now one of the fastest growing fields of academic research in our universities today.

At Duke University, Dr. Joseph B. Rhine took up the study of extrasensory perception in the 1930s and championed it to the point where a department of parapsychology was established at the university. He became its pioneering professor. Today scientists are probing every conceivable frontier for ESP possibilities. Its line-up of protagonists reads like a *Who's Who*. Not only is serious intellectual and scientific study being carried on, but the subject is immensely popular because many of its aggressive proponents profess to be non-religious. It has gained even more widespread respectability in communist societies (such as in the Soviet Union) than here in the United States. It plays the role of a "substitute religion" in some cases, although it has been used primarily as a technique to influence people.

Notice also the reaction on network talk shows. When a celebrity steps through the grand entrance and strolls to the guest chair, he is asked, "Do you believe in ESP?" To say, "No," in the middle 1970s would be as unfashionable as to have said, "Yes," a generation ago. One of the astronauts, Edgar Mitchell, has become such an enthusiastic protagonist of ESP that he now spends full time exploring these frontiers, publishing books, going on talk shows and appearing constantly before the public to talk on this theme.

Why I Wrote This Book

But why write a book on angels? Isn't talking about angels merely adding to the speculation about supernatural phenomena? What possible value is there in such a discussion? Didn't the fascination with angels vanish with the Middle Ages?

Because all the powers of the evil world system seem to be preying on the minds of people already disturbed and frustrated in our generation, I believe the time has come to focus on the positives of the Christian faith. John the Apostle said, "greater is he that is in you, than he that is in the world" (I John 4:4). Satan is indeed capable of doing supernatural things—but he acts only by the permissive will of God; he is on a leash. It is God who is all powerful. It is God who is omnipotent. God has provided Christians with both offensive and defensive weapons. We are not to be fearful; we are not to be distressed; we are not to be deceived; nor are we to be intimidated. Rather, we are to be on our guard, calm and alert "Lest Satan should get an advantage of us, for we are not ignorant of his devices" (II Corinthians 2:11).

One of Satan's sly devices is to divert our minds

from the help God offers us in our struggles against the forces of evil. However, the Bible testifies that God has provided assistance for us in our spiritual conflicts. We are not alone in this world! The Bible teaches us that God's Holy Spirit has been given to empower us and guide us. In addition, the Bible—in nearly three hundred different places—also teaches that God has countless angels at His command. Furthermore, God has commissioned these angels to aid His children in their struggles against Satan. The Bible does not give as much information about them as we might like, but what it does say should be a source of comfort and strength for us in every circumstance.

I am convinced that these heavenly beings exist and that they provide unseen aid on our behalf. I do not believe in angels because someone has told me about a dramatic visitation from an angel, impressive as such rare testimonies may be. I do not believe in angels because UFOs are astonishingly angel-like in some of their reported appearances. I do not believe in angels because ESP experts are making the realm of the spirit world seem more and more plausible. I do not believe in angels because of the sudden worldwide emphasis on the reality of Satan and demons. I do not believe in angels because I have ever seen one—because I haven't.

I believe in angels because the Bible says there are angels; and I believe the Bible to be the true Word of God.

I also believe in angels because I have sensed their presence in my life on special occasions.

So what I have to say in the chapters that follow will not be an accumulation of my ideas about the spirit world, nor even a reflection of my own spiritual experiences in the spirit realm. I propose to put forward, at least in part, what I understand the Bible to say about angels. Naturally, this will not be an exhaustive study of the subject. I hope, however, that it will arouse your curiosity sufficiently for you to dig out from the Bible all that you can find on this subject after you have read this book.

Spiritual forces and resources are available to all Christians. Because our resources are unlimited, Christians will be winners. Millions of angels are at God's command and at our service. The hosts of heaven stand at attention as we make our way from earth to glory, and Satan's BB guns are no match for God's heavy artillery. So don't be afraid. God is for you. He has committed His angels to wage war in the conflict of the ages—and they will win the victory. The Apostle Paul has said in Colossians 2:15, "And having spoiled principalities and powers, he made a show of them openly, triumphing over them." Victory over the flesh, the world and the devil is ours now! The angels are here to help and they are prepared for any emergency.

As you read this book, therefore, I pray that God will open your eyes to the resources He has provided for all who turn to Him for strength. I pray also that God will use it to show you your constant need of Him, and how He has sent His Son, Jesus Christ, into the world to deliver you from both the guilt and power of sin.

CHAPTER 2

Angels Are for Real

I have never heard anyone preach a sermon on angels.

As I have recently tried to correct this in my own ministry, I've asked myself, why this oversight? Why have we ignored the great biblical teachings about angels? In his book, *The Spirit World*, the former New York *Times* reporter Mc-Candlish Phillips asserts that confident belief in the supernatural proceeds from God to men, but never runs the other way. He later makes this distinction: "The initiative in scientific discovery lies wholly with man. The initiative in spiritual revelation lies wholly with God. Men can know only what God elects to reveal to them about the spiritual and the supernatural . . . We can know nothing about angels . . . apart from revelation."

Yet through revelation in the Bible God has told us a great deal. For this reason, theologians through the ages have universally agreed about the importance of "angelology" (the orderly statement of biblical truth about angels). They judged it worthy of treatment in any book of systematic theology. They wrote at length, distinguishing between good angels and satanology (the study of fallen and thus evil angels). But today we have neglected the theme of good angels, although many are giving the devil and all of his demons rapt attention, even worshiping them.

Angels belong to a uniquely different dimension of creation which we, limited to the natural order, can scarcely comprehend. In this angelic domain the limitations are different from those God has imposed on our natural order. He has given angels higher knowledge, power and mobility than us. Have you ever seen or met one of these superior beings called angels? They are God's messengers whose chief business is to carry out His orders in the world. He has given them an ambassadorial charge. He has designated and empowered them as holy deputies to perform works of righteousness. In this way they assist Him as their creator while He sovereignly controls the universe. So He has given them the capacity to bring His holy enterprises to a successful conclusion.

Angels Are Created Beings

Don't believe everything you hear about angels! Some would have us believe that they are only spiritual will-o'-the-wisps. Some view them as only celestial beings with beautiful wings and bowed heads. Others would have us think of them as feminine weirdos.

The Bible states that angels, like men, were created by God. At one time no angels existed; indeed there was nothing but the Triune God: Father, Son and Holy Spirit. Paul, in Colossians 1:16, says, "For by him were all things created, that are in heaven, and that are in earth, visible and invisible." Angels indeed are among the invisible things made by God, for "all things were created by him, and for him." This Creator, Jesus, "is before all things, and by him all things consist" (Colossians 1:17), so that even angels would cease to exist if Jesus, who is Almighty God, did not sustain them by His power.

It seems that angels have the ability to change their appearance and shuttle in a flash from the capital glory of heaven to earth and back again. Although some interpreters have said that the phrase "sons of God" in Genesis 6:2 refers to angels, the Bible frequently makes it clear that angels are non-material; Hebrews 1:14 calls them ministering "spirits." Intrinsically, they do not possess physical bodies, although they may take on physical bodies when God appoints them to special tasks. Further, God has given them no ability to reproduce, and they neither marry nor are given in marriage (Mark 12:25).

The empire of angels is as vast as God's creation. If you believe the Bible, you will believe in their ministry. They crisscross the Old and New

Testaments, being mentioned directly or indirectly nearly three hundred times. As to their number, David recorded 20,000 coursing through the skyways of the stars. Even with his limited vision he impressively notes, "The chariots of God are twenty thousand, even thousands of angels" (Psalm 68:17). Matthew Henry says of this passage, "Angels are 'the chariots of God,' his chariots of war, which he makes use of against his enemies, his chariots of conveyance, which he sends for his friends, as he did for Elijah . . . , his chariots of state, in the midst of which he shows his glory and power. They are vastly numerous: 'Twenty thousands,' even thousands multiplied."

Ten thousand angels came down on Mount Sinai to confirm the holy presence of God as He gave the Law to Moses (Deuteronomy 33:2). An earthquake shook the mountain. Moses was held in speech-bound wonder at this mighty cataclysm attended by the visitation of heavenly beings. Furthermore, in the New Testament John tells us of having seen ten thousand times ten thousand angels ministering to the Lamb of God in the throne room of the universe (Revelation 5:11). The book of Revelation also says that armies of angels will appear with Jesus at the Battle of Armageddon when God's foes gather for their final defeat. Paul in II Thessalonians says, "the Lord Jesus shall be revealed from heaven with his mighty angels" (1:7).

Think of it! Multitudes of angels, indescribably mighty, performing the commands of heaven!

Some biblical scholars believe that angels can be numbered potentially in the millions since Hebrews 12:22 speaks of "an innumerable [myriads —a great but indefinite number] company of angels." More amazingly, even one angel is indescribably mighty, as though an extension of the arm of God. Singly or corporately, angels are for real. They are better organized than were the armies of Alexander the Great, Napoleon or Eisenhower. From earliest antiquity, when the angel guardians of the gates to the glory of Eden sealed the entrance to the home of Adam and Eve, angels have manifested their presence in the world. God placed angelic sentinels called cherubim at the east of the Garden of Eden. They were commissioned not only to bar man's return into Eden, but with "a flaming sword which turned every way, to guard the way to the tree of life" (Genesis 3:24 RSV) lest Adam by eating of its fruit should live forever. If Adam had lived in his sin forever— this earth would long ago have been hell. Thus, in one sense death is a blessing to the human race.

Angels Serve God and Regenerate Men

Witness the unprecedented and unrepeated pageantry at Mt. Sinai. When God moves toward man, it is an event of the first magnitude and can include the vistation of angelic hosts. In the billowing clouds that covered Sinai an angelic trumpeter announced the presence of God. The whole moun-

tain seemed to pulsate with life. Consternation
gripped the people below. The earth seemed con-
vulsed with a nameless fear. As God came to the
mountaintop, He was accompanied by thousands
of angels. Moses, the silent, lone witness, must
have been overcome with even a limited vision of
the forces of God. It staggers the imagination to
wonder what kind of a headline would be
prompted in the daily press for even a man-sided
view of such a heavenly visitation. "And so terrible
was the sight, that Moses said, I exceedingly fear
and quake" (Hebrews 12:21).

The appearance of God was glorious. He shone
like the sun when it goes to its strength. Matthew
Henry, in his commentary, says, "Even Seir and
Paran, two mountains at some distance, were illu-
minated by the divine glory which appeared on
Mount Sinai, and reflected some of the rays of it,
so bright was the appearance, and so much taken
notice to set forth the wonders of the divine
providence (Habakkuk 3:3, 4; Psalm 18:7–9).
The Jerusalem Targum has a strange gloss [note
of explanation] upon this, that, 'when God came
down to give the law, he offered it on Mount Seir
to the Edomites, but they refused it, because they
found in it, *Thou shalt not kill.* Then he offered it
on Mount Paran to the Ishmaelites, but they also
refused it, because they found in it, *Thou shalt not
steal;* and then he came to Mount Sinai and offered it to Israel, and they said, *All that the Lord
shall say we will do.*'" This account by the Jerusalem Targum is, of course, fictional, but it throws

35

an interesting light on how some Jews later regarded this extraordinary and spectacular event.

Belief in Angels: a General Phenomenon

The history of virtually all nations and cultures reveals at least some belief in angelic beings. Ancient Egyptians made the tombs of their dead more impregnable and lavish than their homes because they felt angels would visit there in succeeding ages. Islamic scholars have proposed that at least two angels are assigned to each person: one angel records the good deeds and the other the bad. In fact, long before Islam arose, and even apart from contact with Scripture, some religions taught the existence of angels. But no matter what the traditions, our frame of reference must be the Scripture as our supreme authority on this subject.

Today some hard-nosed scientists lend credence to the scientific probability of angels when they admit the likelihood of unseen and invisible intelligences. Increasingly, our world is being made acutely aware of the existence of occult and demonic powers. People pay attention as never before to sensational headlines promoting such books as *Chariots of the Gods*, *Gods from Outer Space*, *Worlds in Collision*, and movies such as *The Godfather*, *Rosemary's Baby*, and *The Exorcist*. Ought not Christians, grasping the eternal dimension of life, become conscious of the sinless angelic powers who are for real, and who associate with God Himself and administer His works in our behalf? After all, references to the holy angels in the Bible far outnumber references to Satan and his subordinate demons.

Cosmic Powers

If the activities of the devil and his demons seem to be intensifying in these days, as I believe they are, should not the incredibly greater supernatural powers of God's holy angels be even more indelibly impressed on the minds of people of faith? Certainly the eye of faith sees many evidences of the supernatural display of God's power and glory. God is still in business too.

Christians must never fail to sense the operation of angelic glory. It forever eclipses the world of demonic powers, as the sun does the candle's light.

If you are a believer, expect powerful angels to accompany you in your life experiences. And let those events dramatically illustrate the friendly presence of "the holy ones," as Daniel calls them.

Angels speak. They appear and reappear. They feel with apt sense of emotion. While angels may become visible by choice, our eyes are not constructed to see them ordinarily any more than we can see the dimensions of a nuclear field, the structure of atoms, or the electricity that flows through copper wiring. Our ability to sense reality is limited: The deer of the forest far surpass our human capacity in their keenness of smell. Bats possess a phenomenally sensitive built-in radar system. Some animals can see things in the dark that escape our attention. Swallows and geese possess sophisticated guidance systems that appear to border on the supernatural. So why should we think it strange if men fail to perceive the evidences of angelic presence? Could it be that God granted Balaam and his ass a new optical capacity to view the angel? (Numbers 22:23, 31.) Without this special sense they might have thought him to be only a figment of their imagination.

Reports continually flow to my attention from many places around the world telling of visitors of the angelic order appearing, ministering, fellowshiping and disappearing. They warn of God's impending judgment; they spell out the tenderness of His love; they meet a desperate need; then they are gone. Of one thing we can be sure: angels never draw attention to themselves but ascribe glory to God and press His message upon the hearers as a delivering and sustaining word of the highest order.

Demonic activity and Satan worship are on the increase in all parts of the world. The devil is alive and more at work than at any other time. The Bible says that he realizes his time is short, his activity will increase. Through his demonic influences he does succeed in turning many away from the true faith; but we can still say that his evil activities are countered for the people of God by His ministering spirits, the holy ones of the angelic order. They are vigorous in delivering the heirs of salvation from the stratagems of evil men. They cannot fail.

Believers, look up—take courage. The angels are nearer than you think. For after all, God has given "his angels charge of you, to guard you in all your ways. On their hands they will bear you up, lest you dash your foot against a stone" (Psalm 91:11, 12 RSV).

CHAPTER 3

Angels Visible or
Invisible?

The spirit world and its activities are big news today. And the idea of the supernatural is not only seriously regarded, but is accepted as a fact. Many of the most recent books on the subject border on the sensational, or are purely speculative, or have been dreamed up in somebody's imagination. But those who take the Bible at full value cannot discount the subject of angels as speculation or hollow conjecture. After all, the Scriptures mention their existence almost three hundred times.

Have You Ever Seen an Angel?

I have already said that angels are created spirit beings who can become visible when necessary. They can appear and disappear. They think, feel, will and display emotions. But some people have questions about them that ought not concern us. The old debate about how many angels can dance on the point of a needle is foolish. And to ask how many angels can be crowded into a telephone booth or into a Volkswagen hardly merits our attention. On the other hand, we should know what the Bible teaches about them as oracles of God, who give divine or authoritative decisions and bring messages from God to men. In order to fulfill this function angels have not infrequently assumed visible, human form. The writer to the Hebrews asks, "Are they [angels] not all ministering spirits?" Now, have you ever seen a pure spirit? I can't say that I have. Yet I do know that down through the ages God has chosen to manifest His own spiritual presence in different ways. At the baptism of Jesus, God the Holy Spirit was present in the form of a dove. So God has chosen also to manifest His presence through His angels, lesser beings to whom He has given the power to assume forms that make them visible to men.

Are Angels to Be Worshiped?

It is no mere accident that angels are usually invisible. Though God in His infinite wisdom does not, as a rule, permit angels to take on physical dimensions, people tend to venerate them in a fashion that borders on worship. We are warned against worshiping the creature rather than the

Creator (Romans 1:24–25). It's no less than heretical, and indeed is a breach of the first commandment, to worship any manifestation of angelic presence, patron or blesser.

Paul has pointed out that while unusual manifestations may be deeply significant, Jesus Christ the incarnate God, the second person of the Trinity, who is creator of all things and by whom all things exist, is worthy of our worship (Colossians 2:18). We do not pray to angels. Nor are we to engage in "a voluntary humility and worshiping" of them. Only the Triune God is the object of our worship and of our prayers.

Moreover, we should not confuse angels, whether visible or invisible, with the Holy Spirit, the third person of the Trinity and Himself God. Angels do not indwell men, the Holy Spirit seals them and indwells them when He has regenerated them. The Holy Spirit is all knowing, all present, and all powerful. Angels are mightier than men, but they are not gods and they do not possess the attributes of the Godhead.

Not angels, but the Holy Spirit convicts men of sin, righteousness and judgment (John 16:7). He reveals and interprets Jesus Christ to men, while angels remain messengers of God who serve men as ministering spirits (Hebrews 1:14). So far as I know, no Scripture says that the Holy Spirit ever manifested Himself in human form to men. Jesus did this in the incarnation. The glorious Holy Spirit can be everywhere at the same time, but no angel can be in more than one place at any given moment. We know the Holy Spirit as spirit, not flesh, but we can know angels not as spirits alone but sometimes also in visible form.

God uses angels to work out the destinies of men and nations. He has altered the courses of the busy political and social arenas of our society and directed the destinies of men by angelic visitation many times over. We must be aware that angels keep in close and vital contact with all that is happening on the earth. Their knowledge of earthly matters exceeds that of men. We must attest to their invisible presence and unceasing labors. Let us believe that they are here among us. They may not laugh or cry with us, but we do know they delight with us over every victory in our evangelistic endeavors. Jesus taught that "there is joy in the presence of the angels of God when one sinner repents" (Luke 15:10 Living Bible).

Angels Visible? Invisible?

In Daniel 6:22 we read, "My God hath sent his angel, and hath shut the lions' mouths." In the den, Daniel's sight evidently perceived the angelic presence, and the lions' strength more than met its match in the power of the angel. In most instances, angels, when appearing visibly, are so glorious and impressively beautiful as to stun and amaze men who witness their presence.

Can you imagine a being, white and dazzling as lightning? General William Booth, founder of the Salvation Army, describes a vision of angelic beings, stating that every angel was surrounded with an aurora of rainbow light so brilliant that were it not withheld, no human being could stand the sight of it.

Who can measure the brilliance of the lightning flash that illuminates the countryside for miles around? The angel who rolled away the stone from the tomb of Jesus was not only dressed in white, but shone as a flash of lightning with dazzling brilliance (Matthew 28:3). The keepers of the tomb shook and became as dead men. Incidentally, that stone weighed several times more than a single man could move, yet the physical power of the angel was not taxed in rolling it aside.

Abraham, Lot, Jacob and others had no difficulty recognizing angels when God allowed them to manifest themselves in physical form. Note, for example, Jacob's instant recognition of angels in Genesis 32:1,2. "And Jacob went on his way, and the angels of God met him. And when Jacob saw them, he said, This is God's host: and he called the name of that place Mahanaim."

Further, both Daniel and John described the glories of the angels (Daniel 10:6 and Revelation 10:1) visibly descending from heaven with unmeasurable beauty and brilliance, shining like the sun. Who has not thrilled to read the account of the three Hebrew children, Shadrach, Meshach, and Abednego? They refused to fall in tune with the music of obeisance and worship to the king of Babylon. They learned that the angel presence can be observed on occasion by people in the unbelieving world on the outside. After they had refused to bow, the angel preserved them from being burned alive or even having the smell of smoke on their garments from the seventimes-hotter fire. The angel came to them in the midst of the flame without harm and was seen by the king who said, "I see four men . . . in the midst of the fire" (Daniel 3:25).

On the other hand, the Bible indicates angels are more often invisible to human eyes. Whether visible or invisible, however, God causes his angels to go before us, to be with us, and to follow after us. All of this can be fully understood only by believers who know that angelic presences are in control of the battlefield about us, so that we may stand (Isaiah 26:3) with complete confidence in the midst of the fight. "If God be for us who can be against us?"

What Do You See When You See an Angel?

God is forever imaginative, colorful and glorious in what He designs. Some of the descriptions of angels, including the one of Lucifer in Ezekiel 28, indicate that they are exotic to the human eye and mind. Apparently angels have a beauty and variety that surpass anything known to men.

Scripture does not tell us what elements make up angels. Nor can modern science, which is only beginning to explore the realm of the unseen, tell us about the constitution or even the work of angels.

The Bible seems to indicate that they do not age, and never says that one was sick. Except for those who fell with Lucifer, the ravages of sin that have brought destruction, sickness and chaos to our earth have not affected them. The holy angels will never die.

The Bible also teaches that angels are sexless. Jesus said that in heaven men "neither marry, nor are given in marriage, but are as the angels of God in heaven" (Matthew 22:30). This may indicate that angels enjoy relationships that are far more thrilling and exciting than sex. The joy of sex in this life may be only a foretaste of something that believers will enjoy in heaven which is far beyond anything man has ever known.

How are we to understand "theophanies"? (This is a theological term for the visible appearances of Jesus Christ in other forms prior to His incarnation.) Some places in the Old Testament tell us that the second person of the Trinity appeared and was called either "the Lord" or "the angel of the Lord." Nowhere is it clearer than in Genesis 18 where three men appear before Abraham. "Their leader is clearly identified with the Lord, whereas the other two are merely angels. There are no grounds for questioning the very early and traditional Christian interpretation that in these cases there is a preincarnation manifestation of the second person of the Trinity, whether He is called 'the Lord' or 'the Angel of the Lord'" (*Zondervan Pictorial Encyclopedia of the Bible*).

We must remember, then, that in some cases in the Old Testament God Himself appeared in human form as an angel. This reinforces the idea of the relationship between God and His angels. Nevertheless, in almost all of the cases where angelic personages appear they are God's created angelic beings and not God Himself.

CHAPTER 4

Angels—How They Differ from Man

The Bible tells us that God has made man "a little lower than the angels." Yet it also says angels are "ministering spirits, sent forth to minister for them who shall be heirs of salvation" (Hebrews 2:5–7; 1:13, 14). This sounds like a contradiction: man lower—but eventually higher through redemption. How can we explain this?

First we must remember that this Scripture is speaking both of Jesus Christ and men. Jesus did "stoop" when He became man. And as man He was a little lower than the angels in His humanity. But it also speaks about men other than Jesus. God has made men head over all the creatures of our earth world; but they are lower than angels with respect to their bodies and to their place while here on earth. Yet God commands angels to help men since they will be made higher than the angels at the resurrection. So says Jesus in Luke 20:36. God will alter the temporary lower position of man when the kingdom of God has come in its fullness. Now let us examine in detail how God says angels differ from men.

Although angels are glorious beings, the Scriptures make it clear that they differ from regenerated men in significant ways. How can the angels who have never sinned fully understand what it means to be delivered from sin? How can they understand how precious Jesus is to those for whom His death on Calvary brings light, life and immortality? Is it not stranger still that angels themselves will be judged by believers who were once sinners? Such judgment, however, apparently applies only to those fallen angels who followed Lucifer. Thus Paul writes in I Corinthians 6:3, "Know ye not that we shall judge angels?" But even the holy angels have limitations, though the Bible speaks of them as being superior to men in many ways.

Is God "Father" to Angels?

God is not called "Father" by the holy angels because, not having sinned, they need not be redeemed. And the fallen angels cannot call God "Father" because they cannot be redeemed. The latter case is one of the mysteries of Scripture: God made provision for the salvation of fallen men, but He made no provision for the salvation of fallen angels. Why? Perhaps because, unlike Adam and Eve, who were enticed toward sin by sinners, the angels fell when there were no sinners, so no one could entice them to sin. Thus, their sinful state cannot be altered; their sin cannot be forgiven; their salvation cannot be achieved.

The wicked angels would never want to call God "Father," though they may call Lucifer "father," as many Satan worshipers do. They are in revolt against God and will never voluntarily accept His sovereign lordship, except in that Day of Judgment when every knee will bow and every tongue confess that Jesus Christ is Lord (Philippians 2:9, 10). Yet even holy angels who might like to call God "Father" could do so only in the looser sense of that word. As creator, God is the father of all created beings; since angels are created beings, they might think of Him this way. But the term is normally reserved in Scripture for lost men who have been redeemed. So in a real sense, even ordinary men cannot call God "Father" except as their creator God—until they are born again.

Angels Are Not Heirs of God

Christians are joint heirs with Jesus Christ through redemption (Romans 8:17), which is made theirs by faith in Him based on His death at Calvary. Angels who are not joint heirs must stand aside when the believers are introduced to their boundless, eternal riches. The holy angels, however, who are ministering spirits, have never lost their original glory and spiritual relationship with God. This assures them of their exalted place in the royal order of God's creation. By contrast, Jesus identified Himself with fallen men in the incarnation when He was "made a little lower than the angels for the suffering of death" (Hebrews 2:9). That He chose to taste the death we deserve also shows that the holy angels do not share our sinfulness—nor our need of redemption.

Angels Cannot Testify of Salvation by Grace Through Faith

Who can comprehend the overwhelming thrill of fellowship with God and the joy of salvation that even angels do not know? When the local church assembles as a group of Christian believers, it represents in the human sphere the highest order of the love of God. No love could go deeper, rise higher, or extend farther than the amazing love that moved Him to give His only begotten Son. The angels are aware of that joy (Luke 15:10), and when a person accepts God's gift of eternal life through Jesus Christ, angels set all the bells of heaven in motion with their rejoicing before the Lamb of God.

Yet although the angels rejoice when men are saved and glorify God who has saved them, they cannot do one thing: testify personally to something they have not experienced. They can only point to the experiences of the redeemed and rejoice that God has saved such men. This means that throughout eternity men alone will give their personal witness to the salvation that God achieved by grace and that we received through faith in Jesus Christ. The man who has never married cannot fully appreciate the wonders of that relationship. The person who has never lost a father or mother cannot understand what that loss means. So angels, great as they are, cannot testify to salvation the same way as those who have experienced it.

Angels Have No Experiential Knowledge of the Indwelling God

Nothing in the Bible indicates that the Holy Spirit indwells angels as He does redeemed people. Since He seals believers when they accept Christ, such sealing would be unnecessary for the angels who never fell and who therefore need no salvation.

But there is a second reason for this difference. Redeemed men on earth have not yet been glorified. Once God has declared them just and given them life, He embarks on a process of making them inwardly holy while they live here below. At death He makes them perfect. So the Holy Spirit takes His abode in the hearts of all believers while they are still on earth, to perform

52

His unique ministry, one that angels cannot perform. God the Father sent Jesus the Son to die; Jesus performed His unique ministry as His part of God's saving process. Likewise, the Holy Spirit has a role, one different from the Son's. Sent by the Father and the Son, He not only guides and directs believers, but also performs a work of grace in their hearts, conforming them to the image of God to make them holy like Christ. Angels cannot provide this sanctifying power.

Furthermore, angels themselves do not need the ministry of the Holy Spirit the way believers do. The angels have already been endowed with authority by virtue of their relationship to God through creation and continuing obedience. They are unspoiled by sin. Men, however, are not yet perfect and therefore need what the Holy Spirit alone can give. Someday man will be as perfect as angels are now.

Angels Do Not Marry or Procreate

I have already said that angels do not marry. In Matthew 22:30, Jesus points out that "in the resurrection they [men] neither marry, nor are given in marriage, but are as the angels of God in heaven." Because of this we can make a deduction: The number of angels remains constant. For the obedient angels do not die. The fallen angels will suffer the final judgment at the time God finishes dealing with them. While we cannot be certain, some scholars estimate that as many as one third of the angels cast their lot with Satan when he mysteriously rebelled against his creator. In any event the book of Hebrews says the angels constitute an "innumerable company," vast hosts that stagger our imagination. A third of them would likely be counted in the hundreds of thousands—ones who are now desperate demons.

Just as angels differ from men with respect to marriage, so they differ in other important ways. Nothing in Scripture says that angels must eat to stay alive. But the Bible says that on certain occasions angels in human form did indeed eat. David refers to the manna eaten by the children of Israel in the wilderness as the bread of angels. In Psalm 78:25, Asaph says, "Man did eat angels' food." We can hardly disregard what happened to Elijah after he won a great victory over the priests of Baal on Mount Carmel. Because Jezebel threatened his life he needed help from God. So God's angel came to the tired, discouraged prophet and set before him food and drink. When he had eaten twice he was sent on his journey; the food he had eaten was enough to keep him for forty days and forty nights (I Kings 19:5). Not without reason some have concluded that Elijah indeed ate angels' food.

When Abraham was encamped in the plains of Mamre, three angels visited him, of whom one may have been the Lord Jesus (Genesis 18:1, 2). These heavenly beings ate and drank what he provided for them by way of customary entertainment. Shortly thereafter, when God decided to destroy Sodom and Gomorrah, two angelic beings came to save backslidden Lot and his family. Lot made them a feast and there again they ate food, including unleavened bread (Genesis 19).

It is interesting that after His resurrection, Jesus ate with His disciples. Luke's account says that the disciples "gave him a piece of a broiled fish, and of an honeycomb. And he took it, and did eat before them" (Luke 24:42, 43).

The Knowledge of Angels

Angels excel humankind in their knowledge. When King Solomon was being urged to bring Absalom back to Jerusalem, Joab asked a woman of Tekoah to talk to the king. She said: "My lord is wise, according to the wisdom of an angel of God, to know all things that are in the earth" (II Samuel 14:20). And angels possess knowledge that men do not have. But however vast is their knowledge, we can be sure they are not omniscient. They do not know everything. They are not like God. Jesus bore testimony to the limited knowledge of the angels when He was speaking of His second coming. In Mark 13:32 He said, "But of that day and that hour knoweth no man, no, not the angels which are in heaven."

Angels probably know things about us that we do not know about ourselves. And because they are ministering spirits, they will always use this knowledge for our good and not for evil purposes. In a day when few men can be trusted with secret information, it is comforting to know that angels will not divulge their great knowledge to hurt us. Rather, they will use it for our good.

The Power of Angels

Angels enjoy far greater power than men, but they are not omnipotent or "all powerful." Paul in II Thessalonians 1:7 refers to the "mighty angels of God." From the word translated "mighty," here we get the English word "dynamite." In material power, angels are God's dynamite!

In Peter we read, "angels who are greater in might and power [than men] do not bring a reviling judgment against them before the Lord" (II Peter 2:11 NASB). Peter's testimony here reinforces Paul's. We should also note that it took only one angel to slay the first born of Egypt in Moses' day, and one to shut the lions' mouths for Daniel.

In Psalm 103:20 David speaks about [God's] "angels that excel in strength." Nowhere in Scripture is that strength manifested more dramatically than in the climax of this age. Following the Battle of Armageddon, Scripture pictures what will happen to Satan: He is to be bound and cast into a bottomless pit. But what power, apart from God Himself, can do this to Satan, whose power we all know about and whose evil designs we have experienced? The Bible says that one angel will come from heaven. He will have a great chain in his hand. He will lay hold of Satan and bind him with that chain. And then he will cast him into the pit. How great is the power of one of God's mighty angels.

Do Angels Sing?

There has been much conjecture about angel choirs. We at least assume that angels can and do sing, even if the Scriptures do not pointedly say so. In *Hamlet,* William Shakespeare seemed to underscore the possibility that angels sing when he stated, "Now cracks a noble heart, Good night, sweet prince:/and flights of angels sing thee to thy rest."

Some Bible students insist that angels do not sing. This seems inconceivable. Angels possess the ultimate capacity to offer praise, and their music from time immemorial has been the primary vehicle of praise to our all-glorious God. Music is the universal language. It is likely that John saw a massive heavenly choir (Revelation 5:11, 12) of many millions who expressed their praise of the heavenly Lamb through magnificent music. I believe angel choirs will sing in eternity to the glory of God and the supreme delight of the redeemed.

While it is partly speculative, I believe that angels have the capacity to employ heavenly celestial music. Many dying believers have testified that they have heard the music of heaven. Most of my close friends tease me because I cannot carry a tune. When I am singing beside people in a congregation I usually throw them off key. But from years of listening I recognize good music when I hear it even if I can't produce it myself. And there have been times when I have seriously tried to understand and appreciate music I did not like, whether it was a difficult opera or rock. I think before we can understand the music of heaven we will have to go beyond our earthly concept of music. I think most earthly music will seem to us to have been in the "minor key" in comparison to what we are going to hear in heaven.

The Bible tells us of many who sing: Moses (Exodus 15:1), Miriam (Exodus 15:20, 21), David (Psalms), and many others. Thousands of worshipers at the temple continually sang, praising the Lord (II Chronicles 5:12). Thousands of singers preceded the ark of the covenant (I Chronicles 15:27, 28). We all think of Psalms as the hymn book of the Bible.

New Testament believers also sang with rapturous joy. Though the Bible does not say it, it implies that angels, who are of a higher creative order, are tuned to sing with no discordant note to God and the Lamb. Paul reminds us that there is a language of man and a language of angels

58

(I Corinthians 13:1). Angels have a celestial language and make music that is worthy of the God who made them. I believe in heaven we will be taught the language and music of the celestial world. The wonderful hymn, "Holy, Holy Is What the Angels Sing," by Johnson Oatman, Jr., and J. Sweney expresses this thought in verse 4:

> So, altho I'm not an angel,
> yet I know that over there
> I will join the blessed chorus
> that the angels cannot share;
> I will sing about my Saviour,
> who upon dark Calvary
> Freely pardoned my transgressions,
> died to set a sinner free.

Angels Worship Before the Throne

Unquestionably angels ascribe honor and glory to the Lamb of God. But angels do not spend all their time in heaven. They are not omnipresent (everywhere present at the same time), so they can be in only one place at a given time. Yet as God's messengers they are busy around the world carrying out God's orders. Is it not, therefore, obvious that when they are engaged in their ministry here they cannot stand before God's throne? But when angels do stand before the throne of God, indeed they worship and adore their creator.

We can look for that future day when angels

will have finished their earthly ministry. Then
they will gather with all the redeemed before the
throne of God in heaven. There they will offer
their praise and sing their songs. In that day the
angels who veiled their faces and stood mute
when Jesus hung on the cross will then ascribe
glory to the Lamb whose work is finished and
whose kingdom has come. The angels may also
stop to listen as the redeemed children of God express their own thanksgiving for salvation. It
may well be true as the hymn writer has said in
verse 3 of the song, "Holy, Holy Is What the
Angels Sing,"

> Then the angels stand and listen,
> For they cannot join that song,
> Like the sound of many waters,
> By that happy, blood-washed throng.

But the children of God will also stop to listen
to the angels. They have their own reasons for
singing, ones that differ from ours. They have
given themselves to the service of God Almighty.
They have had a part in bringing in the kingdom
of God. They have helped the children of God in
difficult circumstances. So theirs shall be a shout
and a song of victory. The cause they represent
has been victorious; the fight they fought is finished; the enemy they met has been conquered;
their wicked companion angels who fell shall
vex them no more. The angels sing a different
song. But they sing; my, how they sing! And I

believe that angels and those of us who have been redeemed will compete with each other for the endless ages of eternity to see who can best ascribe glory and praise to our wonderful God!

CHAPTER 5

Angelic Organization

We cannot study the subject of angels in the Bible without becoming aware of ranks among angelic beings. The evidence shows that they are organized in terms of authority and glory.

Though some see the ranking of celestial powers as conjectural, it seems to follow this pattern: archangels, angels, seraphim, cherubim, principalities, authorities, powers, thrones, might and dominion (Colossians 1:16; Romans 8:37).

Medieval theologians divided angelic beings into nine grades. Some people, however, have asked whether some of these grades—the principalities, authorities, powers, thrones, might and dominion—could not refer to human institutions and human beings. To answer, we must understand Colossians 1:16. Paul is speaking about creation of things both seen and unseen. On this verse Matthew Henry says that Christ "made all things out of nothing, the highest angel in heaven as well as men upon earth. He made the world, the upper and lower world, with all the inhabitants of both. . . . He [Paul] speaks here as if there were several orders of angels: 'Whether thrones, or dominions, or principalities, or powers,' which must signify either different degrees of excellence or different offices and employments." Perhaps any list that ranks angelic beings will err, but we can be sure they differ in power, some having authority others do not possess. While I do not wish to be dogmatic, I think there are different ranks of them and that the list given in Colossians does refer to these celestial personalities.

1. ARCHANGEL

While Scripture designates only Michael as an archangel (Jude 9), we have biblical grounds for believing that before his fall Lucifer was also an archangel, equal or perhaps superior to Michael. The prefix "arch" suggests a chief, principal or great angel. Thus, Michael is now the angel above all angels, recognized in rank to be the first prince of heaven. He is, as it were, the Prime Minister in God's administration of the universe, and is the "angel administrator" of God for judgment. He must stand alone, because the Bible never speaks of archangels, only *the* archangel. His name means "who is like unto the Lord."

In the Old Testament, Michael seems to be identified primarily with Israel as a nation. Thus,

God speaks of Michael as prince of His chosen people, "the great prince which standeth for the children of thy people" (Daniel 12:1). He specially protects and defends God's people whoever they are.

Further, in Daniel he is referred to as, "Michael, your prince" (Daniel 10:21). He is God's messenger of law and judgment. In this capacity he appears in Revelation 12:7–12 leading the armies that battle Satan, the great dragon, and all of his demons. Michael with his angels will be locked in the titanic struggle of the universe at the last conflict of the age, which will mark the defeat of Satan and all forces of darkness. Scripture tells us in advance that Michael will finally be victorious in the battle. Hell will tremble; heaven will rejoice and celebrate!

Bible students have speculated that Michael cast Lucifer and his fallen angels out of heaven, and that Michael enters into conflict with Satan and the evil angels today to destroy their power and to give to God's people the prospect of their ultimate victory.

Michael, the archangel, will shout as he accompanies Jesus at His Second Coming. Not only does he proclaim the matchless and exciting news that Jesus Christ returns, but he speaks the word of life to all who are dead in Christ and who await their resurrection. "For the Lord himself shall descend from heaven with a shout, with the voice of the archangel . . . and the dead in Christ shall rise first" (I Thessalonians 4:16).

2. GABRIEL, GOD'S MESSENGER

"Gabriel," in Hebrew, means "God's hero," or "the mighty one," or "God is great." Scripture frequently refers to him as "the messenger of Jehovah" or "the Lord's messenger." However, contrary to popular opinion and to the poet John Milton, it never calls him an archangel. Yet it refers to his work more often than to Michael's.

Ministry of Gabriel

Gabriel is primarily God's messenger of mercy and promise. He appears four times in the Bible, always bearing good news (Daniel 8:16, 9:21; Luke 1:9, 26). We may question whether he blows a silver trumpet, since this idea arises from folk music and finds only indirect support in Scripture. But the announcements of Gabriel in unfolding the plans, purposes and verdicts of God are of monumental importance.

In Scripture we gain our first glimpse of Gabriel in Daniel 8:15, 16. There he announces the vision of God for the "end time." God has charged him to convey the message from the "situation room" of heaven that reveals God's plan in history. In verse 17 Gabriel says, "Understand, . . . the vision belongs to (events that shall occur in) the time of the end" (Amplified Bible).

Daniel, while in prayer, records Gabriel's second appearance to him: "While I was speaking in prayer, the man Gabriel, whom I had seen in the former vision, being caused to fly swiftly, came near to me and touched me about the time of the evening sacrifice" (Daniel 9:21 Amp.B.). To Daniel he said, "Understand the vision" (9:23), and then revealed to him the magnificent sequence of events at the end time. Gabriel, sketching panoramically the procession of earthly kingdoms, assured Daniel that history would culminate in the return of Christ, "the prince of princes" (Daniel 8:25 Amp.B.) and conqueror of the "king of fierce countenance" (Daniel 8:23 Amp.B.). The prophetic announcement by Daniel in his prayer to God is two-fold. He expressly refers to the more immediate judgment upon Israel (Daniel 9:16) and then to the awesome portent of "end time judgment" and "tribulation" which shall be for "seven years" (Daniel 9:27). In a later chapter, "Angels in Prophecy," we will trace how the angels supervise the fearsome events of the end time.

Gabriel in the New Testament

Gabriel first appears in the New Testament in Luke 1. He identifies himself to Zacharias (verse 19), announces the birth of John the Baptist, and describes his life and ministry as the forerunner of Jesus.

But in his most important appearance, Gabriel informs the Virgin Mary about Jesus, the incarnate God! What a message to deliver to the world through a teen-age girl! What a wonderfully holy girl she must have been, to be visited by the mighty Gabriel. He declares:

> Fear not, Mary: for thou hast found favour with God. And, behold, thou shalt conceive in thy womb, and bring forth a son, and shalt call his name Jesus. . . . And he shall reign over the house of Jacob for ever; and of his kingdom there shall be no end (Luke 1: 30–33).

Throughout all time, this divine declaration of Gabriel shall be the Magna Charta of the incarnation and the foundation stone of the world to come: God became flesh to redeem us.

3. SERAPHIM

It would appear from the Bible that celestial and extraterrestrial beings differ in rank and authority. The seraphim and cherubim follow in order after the archangel and angels. These may possibly define the angelic authority to which Peter refers when he speaks of Jesus, "Who is gone into heaven, and is on the right hand of God; angels and authorities and powers being made subject unto him" (I Peter 3:22).

The word "seraphim" may come from the Hebrew root meaning "love" (though some think the

word means "burning ones" or "nobles"). We
find the seraphim only in Isaiah 6:1–6. It is an
awe-inspiring sight as the worshiping prophet be-
holds the six-winged seraphim above the throne
of the Lord. We can assume that there were several seraphim since Isaiah speaks about "each
one" and "one cried unto another."

The ministry of the seraphim is to praise the
name and character of God in heaven. Their ministry relates directly to God and His heavenly
throne, because they are positioned above the
throne—unlike the cherubim, who are beside it.
Students of the Bible have not always agreed on
the duties of the seraphim, but we know one
thing: they are constantly glorifying God. We
also learn from Isaiah 6:7 that God can use them
to cleanse and purify His servants.

They were indescribably beautiful. "With two
[wings] he covered his face, and with two he
covered his feet, and with two he did fly" (im-
plying that some angelic beings fly). The Scriptures do not, however, support the common belief that all angels have wings. The traditional
concept of angels with wings is drawn from their
ability to move instantaneously and with unlimited speed from place to place, and wings were
thought to permit such limitless movement. But
here in Isaiah 6 only two of the seraphim's wings
were employed for flying.

The glory of the seraphim reminds us of
Ezekiel's description of the four living creatures.

He did not call them seraphim, but they too performed their service for God. Like seraphim they acted as both agents and spokesmen of God. In both cases the glory displayed was a witness to God, though only the seraphim, of course, hovered over the heavenly throne as functionaries and attendants, with a chief duty of praising God. In all these manifestations we see God willing that men should know of His glory. He determines to maintain an adequate witness to that glory in both terrestrial and celestial realms.

4. CHERUBIM

Cherubim are real and they are powerful. But the cherubim in the Bible were often symbolic of heavenly things. "At God's direction they were incorporated into the design of the Ark of the Covenant and the Tabernacle. Solomon's temple utilized them in its decoration" (*Zondervan Pictorial Encyclopedia*). They had wings, feet and hands. Ezekiel 10 pictures the cherubim in detail as having not only wings and hands, but being "full of eyes," encompassed by "wheels within wheels."

But Ezekiel sounds a somber note in chapter 10 also, and the cherubim provide the clue. The prophet presents his vision that prophesies the destruction of Jerusalem. In Ezekiel 9:3, the Lord has descended from His throne above the cherubim to the threshold of the temple, while in 10:1 He returns again to take His seat above them. In the calm before the storm, we see the cherubim stationed on the south side of the sanctuary. Being stationed in position toward the city, they witness the beginning of the gradual withdrawal of God's glory from Jerusalem. The fluttering of their wings indicates immensely important events to follow (10:5). Then the cherubim rise up in preparation for the departure.

While Ezekiel 10 is difficult to understand, one point comes across clearly. The cherubim have to do with the glory of God. This chapter is one of the most mysterious and yet descriptive passages of the glory of God to be found in the Bible, and it involves angelic beings. It should be read carefully and prayerfully. The reader gets a sense of God's greatness and glory as in few other passages in the Bible.

While the seraphim and the cherubim belong to different orders and are surrounded by much mystery in Scripture, they share one thing. They constantly glorify God. We see the cherubim beside the throne of God. "Thou that dwellest between the cherubim, shine forth" (Psalm 80:1). "He sitteth between the cherubim" (Psalm 99:1). God's glory will not be denied, and every heavenly being gives silent or vocal testimony to the splendor of God. In Genesis 3:24, we see cherubim guarding the tree of life in Eden. In the tabernacle in the wilderness designs representing the guardian cherubim formed a part of the mercy seat and were made of gold (Exodus 25:18).

The cherubim did more than guard the most holy place from those who had no right of access to God. They also assured the right of the high priest to enter the holy place with blood as the mediator with God on behalf of the people. He, and he alone, was permitted to enter into the inner sanctuary of the Lord. By right of redemption and in accordance with the position of believers, each true child of God now has direct access as a believer-priest to the presence of God through Jesus. Cherubim will not refuse the humblest Christian access to the throne. They assure us that we can come boldly—because of Christ's work on the cross! The veil in the temple has been rent. As Paul says, "Ye are no more strangers and foreigners, but fellow citizens with the saints, and of the household of God" (Ephesians 2:19). Further, Peter assures that "Ye are a chosen generation, a royal priesthood, an holy nation, a peculiar people; that ye should show forth the praises of him who hath called you out of darkness into his marvellous light" (I Peter 2:9).

The inner sanctuary of God's throne is always open to those who have repented of sin and trusted Christ as Savior.

Many believe that the "living creatures" often mentioned in the book of Revelation are cherubim. But as glorious as the angelic and heavenly beings are, they become dim beside the inexpressible glory resident in our heavenly Lamb, the Lord of glory, to whom all powers in heaven and on earth bow in holy worship and breathless adoration.

CHAPTER 6

Lucifer and the Angelic Rebellion

Few people realize the profound part angelic forces play in human events. It is Daniel who most dramatically reveals the constant and bitter conflict between the holy angels faithful to God and the angels of darkness allied with Satan (Daniel 10:11–14). This Satan, or the devil, was once called "Lucifer, the son of the morning." Along with Michael he may have been one of the two archangels, but he was cast from heaven with his rebel forces, and continues to fight. Satan may appear to be winning the war because sometimes he wins important battles, but the final outcome is certain. One day he will be defeated and stripped of his powers eternally. God will shatter the powers of darkness.

Many people ask, "How could this conflict come about in God's perfect universe?" The Apostle Paul calls it "the mystery of iniquity" (II Thessalonians 2:7). While we have not been given as much information as we might like, we do know one thing for certain: The angels who fell, fell because they had sinned against God. In II Peter 2:4 the Scripture says, "God spared not the angels that sinned but cast them down to hell, and delivered them into chains of darkness, to be reserved unto judgment." Perhaps the parallel passage in Jude 6 puts the onus of responsibility more directly on the shoulders of the angels themselves. "The angels," wrote Jude, quite deliberately, "kept not their first estate, but left their own habitation."

Thus, the greatest catastrophe in the history of the universal creation was Lucifer's defiance of God and the consequent fall of perhaps one third of the angels who joined him in his wickedness.

When did it happen? Sometime between the dawn of creation and the intrusion of Satan into the Garden of Eden. The poet Dante reckoned that the fall of the rebel angels took place within twenty seconds of their creation and originated in the pride that made Lucifer unwilling to await the time when he would have perfect knowledge. Others, like Milton, put the angelic creation and fall immediately prior to the temptation of Adam and Eve in the Garden of Eden.

But the important question is not, "When were angels created?" but, "When did they fall?" It is difficult to suppose that their fall occurred before God placed Adam and Eve in the Garden. We know for a fact that God rested on the seventh day, or at the end of all creation, and pronounced everything to be good. By implication, up to this time even the angelic creation was good. We might then ask, "How long were Adam and Eve in the Garden before the angels fell and before Satan tempted the first man and woman?" This question must remain unanswered. All we can say positively is that Satan, who had fallen before he tempted Adam and Eve, was the agent and bears a greater guilt because there was no one to tempt him when he sinned; on the other hand Adam and Eve were faced with a tempter.

Thus, we pick up the story where it began. It all started mysteriously with Lucifer. He was the most brilliant and most beautiful of all created beings in heaven. He was probably the ruling prince of the universe under God, against whom he rebelled. The result was insurrection and war in heaven! He began a war that has been raging in heaven from the moment he sinned and was brought to earth shortly after the dawn of human history. It sounds like a modern world crisis!

Isaiah 14:12–14 records the conflict's origin. Prior to his rebellion, Lucifer, an angel of light, is described in scintillating terms in Ezekiel 28:12–17 (NASB): "You had the seal of perfection, full of wisdom and perfect in beauty. . . . You were the anointed cherub who covers, and I placed you there. You were on the holy mountain of God. You walked in the midst of the stones of fire. You were blameless in your ways from the day you were created, until unrighteousness was found in you. . . . Your heart was lifted up because of your beauty; you corrupted your wisdom by reason of your splendor." When the angel Lucifer rebelled against God and His works, some have estimated that as many as one third of the angelic hosts of the universe may have joined him in his rebellion. Thus, the war that started in heaven continues on earth and will see its climax at Armageddon with Christ and His angelic army victorious.

Leslie Miller in his excellent little book, *All About Angels*, points out that Scripture sometimes refers to angels as stars. This explains why prior to his fall Satan was called, "the star of the morning." And to this description John adds a qualifying detail, "His tail swept away a third of the stars of heaven and threw them to the earth" (Revelation 12:4 RSV).

Rebellion in Heaven

The Apostle Paul understood and spoke of the war of rebellion in the heavens when he referred to the former Lucifer, now Satan, as "the prince of the power of the air, the spirit that now worketh in the children of disobedience" (Ephesians 2:2). He also says that in fighting the organized kingdom of satanic darkness, we struggle against "the world-forces of this darkness . . . the spiritual forces of wickedness in the heavenly places" (Ephesians 6:12 NASB).

We can describe all unrighteousness and transgression against God as "self-will" against the will of God. This definition applies to human beings today as well as to angels.

Lucifer's Five "I Wills"

Lucifer, the son of the morning, was created, as were all angels, for the purpose of glorifying God. However, instead of serving God and praising Him forever, Satan desired to rule over heaven and creation in the place of God. He wanted supreme authority! Lucifer said (Isaiah 14), "I will ascend into heaven." "I will exalt my throne above the stars of God." "I will sit also upon the mount of the congregation." "I will ascend above the heights of the clouds." "I will be like the most high." I . . . I . . . I . . . I . . . I.

Lucifer was not satisfied with being subordinated to his creator. He wanted to usurp God's throne. He exulted at the thought of being the center of power throughout the universe—he wanted to be the Caesar, the Napoleon, the Hitler of the entire universe. The "I will" spirit is the spirit of rebellion. His was a bold act to dethrone the Lord Most High. Here was a wicked schemer who saw himself occupying the superlative position of power and glory. He wanted to be worshiped, not to worship.

Satan's desire to replace God as ruler of the universe may have been rooted in a basic sin that leads to the sin of pride I have already mentioned. Underneath Satan's pride lurked the deadliest of all sins, the sin of covetousness. He wanted what did not belong to him. Virtually every war ever fought began because of covetousness. The warfare in heaven and on earth between God and the devil certainly sprang from the same desire—the lust for what belonged to God alone.

Today, as always in the past, virtually no one can sin alone. The influences of sin are contagious. The Bible speaks of "the dragon . . . and his angels" (Revelation 12:7), indicating that along with Lucifer, myriads of angels also chose to deny the authority of God and subsequently lost their high position. They chose to participate in the "war program" of Lucifer. As a result of their fall, those angels have been "reserved unto judgment" (II Peter 2:4) and have their part with Lucifer in the "everlasting fire, prepared for the devil and his angels" (Matthew 25:41). But until this happens they constitute a mighty force —capable of wreaking havoc among individuals, families and nations! Watch out, they are dangerous, vicious and deadly. They want you under their control and they will pay any price to get you!

Satan, the fallen prince of heaven, has made his decision to battle against God to the death. He is the master craftsman who has plotted destruction during all the ages since he first rebelled. His "I will" spirit has worked through his consuming hatred of God to write his tragic story in the annals of human history. In his warfare against God, Satan uses the human race, which God created and loved. So God's forces of good and Satan's forces of evil have been engaged in a deadly conflict from the dawn of our history. Unless world leaders and statesmen understand the true nature of this warfare, they will continue to be blind leaders of the blind. They can only patch a little here and patch a little there. We will find no final solution to the world's great problems until this spiritual warfare has been settled. And it will be settled in the last war of history—Armageddon. Then Christ and His angelic armies will be the victor!

Past, Present and Future in Perspective

Lucifer became Satan, the devil, the author of sin; and it is sin that has always deceived, disturbed, betrayed, depraved and destroyed all that it has touched.

Will there never be an end to this Battle of the Ages, this war against God lustfully conceived in Lucifer and perpetrated on earth?

Not only does the battle rage on earth, but it rages in heaven. "And there was war in heaven: Michael and his angels fought against the dragon; and the dragon fought and his angels . . . and the great dragon was cast out" (Revelation 12:7, 9).

Satan and his demons are known by the discord they promote, the wars they start, the hatred they engender, the murders they initiate, the opposition to God and His commandments. They are dedicated to the spirit of destruction. On the other hand the holy angels obey their Creator. No discordant note sounds among the angels of heaven. They are committed to fulfill the purpose for which all true children of God pray, "Thy kingdom come. Thy will be done . . . as it is in heaven" (Matthew 6:10).

The Bible refers to Lucifer and the fallen angels as those who sinned and did not keep their first position (Jude 6). They committed the sins of consummate pride and covetousness. The sin of pride particularly has caused the downfall of many men. If pride could bring about the downfall of Lucifer in heaven, most certainly it can bring mortal man down too. We must be on guard against pride, or we are headed for a fall patterned after the fall of Lucifer and his angels, who turned into demons.

Could it be that God wanted to be sure that men would not question the existence of Satan and his demon-hosts? Perhaps He had this in mind when He inspired the writing of Ezekiel 28, which sets forth the typology of Satan in the earthly sense. This account by the prophet Ezekiel speaks of an earthly prince of the city of Tyre. He seems to be an earthly symbol of Satan. It is clear from the passage that the king of Tyre became a devil incarnate, and an earthly illustra-

tion of the heavenly Lucifer who became the
devil.

We live in a perpetual battlefield—The great
War of the Ages continues to rage. The lines of
battle press in ever more tightly about God's own
people. The wars among nations on earth are
merely popgun affairs compared to the fierce-
ness of battle in the spiritual, unseen world. This
invisible spiritual conflict is waged around us incessantly and unremittingly. Where the Lord
works, Satan's forces hinder; where angel beings
carry out their divine directives, the devils rage.
All this comes about because the powers of darkness press their counterattack to recapture the
ground held for the glory of God.

Were it not for the angel hosts empowered by
God to resist the demons of Satan, who could
ever hope to press through the battlements of the
fiendish demons of darkness to the Lord of eternal liberty and salvation? Paul speaks the truth
when he says that the forts of darkness are impregnable. Yet they yield to the warfare of faith
and light as angel hosts press the warfare to gain
the victory for us (II Corinthians 10:4, 5).

Satan on the Attack

Revelation 12:10 speaks of Satan as "the
accuser of the brethren" and Ephesians 6:12
(RSV) describes the "principalities . . . powers
. . . the darkness of this world . . . the spiritual

hosts of wickedness in the heavenly places." Although Satan and his evil followers press their warfare in the heavens, it seems that their primary endeavor is to destroy faith in the world.

Isaiah 13:12–14 clearly points up Satan's objectives: he works to bring about the downfall of nations, to corrupt moral standards and to waste human resources. Corrupting society's order, he want to prevent the attainment of order, and to shake the kingdoms of our God. He uses his destructive power to create havoc, fire, flood, earthquake, storm, pestilence, disease, and the devastation of peoples and nations. The description of Satan's great power ends with the words, "who opened not the house of his prisoners" (Isaiah 13:17). This undoubtedly refers to the prison house of Satan, Hades or the abode of the dead so clearly pictured in Luke 16:19–31. Satan has great power. He is cunning and clever, having set himself against God and His people. He will do everything in his power to hold people captive in sin and to drag them down to the prison of eternal separation from God.

Since the fall of Lucifer, that angel of light and son of the morning, there has been no respite in the bitter Battle of the Ages. Night and day Lucifer, the master craftsman of the devices of darkness, labors to thwart God's plan of the ages. We can find inscribed on every page of human history the consequences of the evil brought to fruition by the powers of darkness with the devil in charge. Satan never yields an inch, nor does he ever pause in his opposition to the plan of God to redeem the "cosmos" from his control. He forever tries to discredit the truthfulness of the Word of God; he coaxes men to deny the authority of God; and he persuades the world to wallow in the deluding comforts of sin. Sin is the frightful fact in our world. It writes its ruin in vice and lust, in the convulsions of war, in selfishness and sorrow, and in broken hearts and lost souls. It remains as the tragedy of the universe and the tool of Satan to blunt or destroy the works of God.

Satanic Intrigue

God cannot tolerate sin forever if He is just. He will not permit the perversions of Lucifer to mock Him, for the inescapable answer to the evil of the world is found in the unalterable law of the Word of God that "the wages of sin is death; but the gift of God is eternal life through Jesus Christ our Lord" (Romans 6:23). Satan's attacks, which began at the dawn of history, will continue until God begins to bring down the curtain on this frightening drama at Armageddon.

Satan's ideology is based on the little word "if." Through all time he has sought to discredit God by making Him out a liar in the eyes of man. He never ceases trying to discredit the claims of the Word of God and to rob mankind of the strength and comfort of faith. The all-time tool of Lucifer is an "if," but God declares that there are no "ifs," "buts" or "ands" about His program for salvation. God's plan is unalterable; His antidote for the satanic "if" works and is unchangeable. God assures us that through the work of Christ and the labors of His angelic deputies we can look for the triumphant and victorious warfare over the armies of Lucifer.

It is not surprising that the fallen Lucifer hatched his plot to usurp the pre-eminence of God in His creation. In the first conversation in the Garden, the serpent embodying Lucifer asked, "Hath God said, Ye shall not eat of every tree of the garden?" (Genesis 3:1). To this the reply came, "You shall not eat of the fruit of the tree which is in the midst of the garden . . . lest you die" (Genesis 3:3 RSV).

Hear Lucifer reply, if you eat of the fruit of this tree "ye shall not surely die" (Genesis 3:4). He says in effect that God does not know what He is talking about. Satan often works by interjecting a question to raise doubts. It is deadly to doubt God's Word! Satan's strategy is to persuade us to rationalize. Eve probably began to reason with the enemy: Is it possible that God would be so unjust and unkind as to forbid this seemingly innocent thing?—"it was pleasant to the eyes" (Genesis 3:6). Eve foolishly parleyed with the tempter. In her own mind she began to doubt the truth and the wisdom of God. The poisoned tip of sin entered in when she reasoned in her own mind against the wisdom of God.

How easily Satan covers with a light color ideas that are dark. His intrigue comes to us colored in the light of our own desires. Time after time he injects his subtle "ifs." "This tree is to be desired to make one wise." Eve listened; she reasoned with herself, she looked, she touched, she took, she tasted. Satan never fails to appeal to the appetites of the flesh and to the seeming sensual satisfactions that come from the inventions of sin. Our senses are inlets through which Satan can work, prod and inject his deadly "ifs."

The Genesis account states that Eve ate first, and then gave some to Adam to eat. If they had fixed their minds on God and trusted His wisdom, recognizing the danger that lurked in the fruit He had forbidden, all history would have been radically different and had another ending. Had they only realized the consequences of disobedience, had they only seen the danger of the satanic "if," had they only envisioned the flaming sword barring them forever from the Garden! Had they only realized the terrible consequences of a single "innocent" moment, they would not have had to stand over the silent, lifeless form of their son Abel. His tragic death was the fruit of the seductive power of sin in their own lives. Apart from it our world would have been paradise today!

Had Adam and Eve resisted the devil, he would have fled, forever defeated. But they fell, and thus death passed upon all men (Genesis 3:13). This is where death began! Sin works the same with all of us, whatever our condition, nature or environment. We are depraved by nature because we inherited it from our parents (Romans 3:19). The stream has been polluted. We must bear the sentence of guilt and the stain of sin. Each must give account of himself to God.

Listen to Satan's "ifs" of death being injected into the minds of people today: "if" you live a good life, "if" you do what is right, "if" you go to church, "if" you work for the benefit of others— if, if, if. But the Bible teaches that these "ifs" are not enough to meet God's requirements for salvation. Our good works and intentions are not enough. Jesus said, "Ye must be born again" (John 3:7).

These are Satan's approaches today. The hiss of the serpent is the "if" of death. The stench of death is everywhere today! As C. S. Lewis points out, "War does not increase death—death is total in every generation." But we can find eternal life when we believe in Jesus Christ.

CHAPTER 7

The Personal Ministry
of Angels

Angels minister to us personally. Many accounts in Scripture confirm that we are the subjects of their individual concern.

As an evangelist I have often felt too far spent to minister from the pulpit to men and women who have filled stadiums to hear a message from the Lord. Yet again and again my weariness has vanished, and my strength has been renewed. I have been filled with God's power not only in my soul but physically. On many occasions God has become especially real, and has sent His unseen angelic visitors to touch my body to let me be His messenger for heaven, speaking as a dying man to dying men.

We may not always be aware of the presence of angels. We can't always predict how they will appear. But angels have been said to be our neighbors. Often they may be our companions without our being aware of their presence. We know little of their constant ministry. The Bible assures us, however, that one day our eyes will be unscaled to see and know the full extent of the attention angels have given us (I Corinthians 13:11, 12).

Many experiences of God's people suggest that angels have been ministering to them. Others may not have known they were being helped, yet the visitation was real. The Bible tells us that God has ordered angels to minister to His people— those who have been redeemed by the power of Christ's blood.

In the Old Testament, Daniel vividly describes the bitter conflict between the angelic forces of God and the opposing demons of darkness. Before the angel came to him he had spent three weeks mourning (Daniel 10:3). He ate no bread, meat or wine, nor did he anoint himself. As he stood by the Tigris River, a man appeared clothed in linen. His face looked like lightning and his eyes like flaming torches. His voice sounded like the roar of a crowd.

Daniel alone saw the vision. The men who were with him did not. Yet a great dread came upon them, and they ran away to hide. Left alone with the heavenly visitor, Daniel's strength departed from him, so great was the effect of this personage on him.

Daniel was held in the bonds of a great sleep, yet he heard the voice of the angel. A hand touched him and the angel described an experience he himself had just had. The angel had started to come to Daniel from the moment he began to pray, but en route was waylaid by a demon prince who engaged him in conflict and delayed him. Then Michael came to help this subordinate angel, freeing him to fulfill his mission to Daniel.

The angel had a message. He was to show Daniel what God foresaw would befall the world —especially Israel in the latter days. Daniel then found himself weak and unable to speak, so the angel touched his lips and also restored his strength. Having finished his mission, the angel told Daniel he was returning to fight with the demon prince in the unending struggle of the forces of good versus the forces of evil. In all this Daniel was having no hallucination or dream. It was a genuine experience with a real person, and no one could ever have persuaded Daniel otherwise.

He had pleaded with God for the sons of Israel. His prayer session, accompanied by fasting, had lasted for three weeks. At that moment he received the news from the "angel visitor" sent from heaven that his prayer had been heard. This incident makes it clear that delays are not denials, and that God's permissive will is involved in all of life.

During several world crises I have had the privilege of talking with some heads of state or secretaries of state. I recall that during the 1967 Middle East war, Secretary of State Dean Rusk, who was visiting my home town of Montreat, North Carolina, invited me to his room. While we were discussing the war that had just broken out, I told him I believed "supernatural forces are at work."

On the eve of one of his missions abroad during the Ford Administration, Secretary of State Kissinger briefed me on some of the staggering problems facing the world. I told him I believed the world was experiencing an unseen spiritual war in which the powers of darkness were attacking the forces of God. As we have moved through the turbulent events of the past decade, I have become more convinced than ever that the activities of the unseen demonic forces are increasing. A well-known television newscaster said to me in his office, "The world is out of control." It seems incredible that such a warfare is taking place— but the Bible says it is!

Dr. A. C. Gaebelein has called it "the conflict of the ages." It will be resolved only when Jesus Christ returns to earth. This is why the world is crying for "a leader." The Anti-Christ, who will be Satan's "front," will arrive on the scene for a brief time and seemingly be The Answer. But after only a few months the world will be thrown back into chaos and conflict. He will prove to be "The Lie" (II Thessalonians 2:3–10). Then the One whom God chose and anointed before time began will return to earth with His mighty, holy angels. At the end of the age, He will throw the devil and his demons into the lake of fire. Thus, for the true believer the conflict now raging will end as God intends. Righteousness will prevail.

The experience of Jacob with angels is a splendid illustration of their ministry for God to men. In some ways Jacob was a cheat. He had stolen the birthright from his brother. He lied to his father and deceived him when his sight was almost gone. He fled from his brother, who would have killed him. He married his Uncle Laban's two daughters, and when their father and brothers no longer looked on him with favor he took his family and flocks back to Canaan.

Though Jacob was a cunning schemer and skilled in deception, God was concerned for him as the one who was in "the line of promise." From him the twelve tribes of Israel were to come. While he was en route home the Scripture tells us that "the angels of God met him." So overcome was he by what happened that he said, "This is God's Army!" (verse 2, Genesis 32 Amp. B.), and called the place Mahanaim, meaning "two camps." He called the angels, "God's hosts." But the story does not end there. Having formerly cheated his brother Esau, he now feared him, not knowing whether he would be welcomed or killed. So Jacob prayed, admitting he was not worthy of the least of God's mercies. He asked to be delivered from the hand of his brother Esau.

The night before Jacob met Esau he was alone, his family and servants having gone ahead. Suddenly a man appeared and wrestled with him until daybreak, when he finally touched Jacob's thigh, "and the hollow of the thigh was out of joint." At this, Jacob realized the man was a

heavenly visitor, and would not let him go until
the man had blessed him. When he had told the
stranger his name, the man said, "Thy name shall
be called no more Jacob, but Israel: for as a prince
hast thou power with God and with men and hast
prevailed." When Jacob asked the man to identify
himself, he received no reply. But the man blessed
him there. Jacob called the place Peniel, meaning "face of God," saying, "I have seen God face to
face, and my life is preserved" (Genesis 32:24–
30).

It may well be that the wrestler was Jesus, appearing fleetingly in human form. In the former
part of the story many angels were surrounding
Jacob. Through the two experiences, God revealed
His will for Jacob's life more fully, and promised
that he would be a prince. The next day he therefore went forward cheerfully to meet Esau; everything turned out well for him and his family.
Centuries later Hosea testified to this incident,
saying that the God of heaven had appeared to
Jacob, ministering to him in the person of an
angel (Hosea 12:3–6).

Moses and Abraham are perhaps the two
greatest Old Testament characters; angels were
involved in their lives on important occasions.
We have already seen how angels ministered to
Abraham. We must look at the experience of
Moses at the burning bush (Exodus 3).

The background is important. For forty years
Moses had lived amid the splendors of Egypt,
coming to know its language, customs and laws.

He lived a life of luxury and occupied an important position in the social structure. Then because of the misadventure of slaying an Egyptian he fled to the desert. For forty years more he was tutored as a sheepherder in the "university of solitude." Scripture says little about that period, but it represented a great change in circumstances to go from the court of Pharaoh to a field of grazing sheep. It was not exactly an occupation that ranked high in the social order. He was an outcast, a lonely figure compared to his former life. And it took God forty years to bring him to the place where he was serviceable for the job God had in mind for him. So it was that at eighty years of age, when the life work of most people has already been completed, Moses was ready for God's call.

One day as he was going about his duties, Moses saw a bush burning. It struck him as peculiar because the bush was not consumed. More than that, "the angel of the Lord appeared to him in a flame of fire out of the midst of the bush." Since we have no reason to suppose that Moses had ever seen an angel before, this must have been an extraordinary visitation to him. Further, his curiosity was aroused. Then it was that God Himself spoke to Moses out of the bush.

Moses was profoundly moved. Having told him to remove his shoes because he was standing on holy ground, God identified Himself as the God of Abraham, Isaac and Jacob. At this Moses was awestruck, and hid his face, fearing to look at

God. God then disclosed to Moses His plan to release the Israelites from their captivity in Egypt, using Moses as their leader. When asked by Moses whom he should say had told him this when he approached the Israelites, God responded, "say I AM hath sent me unto you."

Moses was not at all enthusiastic about what God told him to do. He began to offer what he thought were compelling reasons to be excused from that service. First he said that the people of Israel would never believe him, and therefore would not accept his leadership. In answer, God asked him what he had in his hand. Moses said, "a rod." "Cast it on the ground," God said, and suddenly it became a serpent. But when he picked it up, it again became a rod. Then at God's command he put his hand in his robe, and withdrawing it found it leprous. But putting it back a second time and withdrawing it, he found it free of all disease. By such signs, God said, would he show the people Moses' divine commission.

Then Moses made another excuse: He said he couldn't talk, professing to be slow of speech. Perhaps this was the result of forty years in virtual silence on the backside of the desert, but God even refused this excuse, saying He would send Aaron to be his voice. And so Moses went from the desert to Egypt to begin the work of deliverance. But the incident is important in our study because it is tied closely to the angel of the Lord in the burning bush. This again shows that

God used angels (or appeared as an angel) to make His will known and communicate His decisions to men.

The presence of angels became part of "the Exodus experience." Thus, in Numbers 20:16 the Bible says, "When we cried unto the Lord, he heard our voice, and sent an angel, and hath brought us forth out of Egypt." Isaiah says that "In all their affliction he was afflicted, and the angel of his presence saved them: in his love and in his pity he redeemed them; and he bare them, and carried them all the days of old" (63:9). It may well be that some of these instances involved angelic forms taken by Jesus Christ, the second person of the Trinity. We can only speculate. In that event, it makes alive the thrilling testimony of Paul who declared that "Jesus Christ [is] the same yesterday, and today, and for ever" (Hebrews 13:8).

Therefore, just as Jesus is with us now through the Holy Spirit, revealing Himself and His will, so was He with His people in ages past, and so shall He be for all time to come, the angel of God's presence who leads us. To His "faithful" of past ages, God the Father revealed His presence through angels; through *the* angel of the Lord, God the Son, Jesus Christ, He revealed Himself and redeemed us by the Son's crucifixion, death and resurrection. Here is mystery too deep for any of us to fathom fully.

Jewish scholars called the angel of the Lord by the name, "Metatron," "the angel of countenance," because He witnesses the countenance of God continuously and, therefore, works to extend the program of God for each of us.

God has given us the fullest revelation—Jesus Christ in the flesh—so He no longer needs to manifest Himself in the form of "the angel of the Lord" in this age of grace. Consequently, the angels who appear in the New Testament or even today are always "created spirits" and not God in that special angel form He used now and then in the Old Testament. The appearance of God the Son in physical form (a theophany) in the Old Testament is no longer necessary. Consider the presence of angels in the New Testament subsequent to the thrilling account of the birth of God the Son in the flesh through His incarnation at Bethlehem. The angels then were to minister the message of God and to establish the message of the gospel of Christ, but never to supplant it or to detract from it.

God uses both men and angels to declare His message to those who have been saved by grace. "Are they [angels] not all ministering spirits, sent forth to minister for them who shall be heirs of salvation?" (Hebrews 1:14.) What a glorious honor it will be for angels to know us by name because of our faithful witness to others. Angels will share our rejoicing over those who repent (Luke 15:10), even though they cannot preach the gospel themselves.

In this regard, consider Philip the deacon, whom God was using as a minister of revival in

Samaria. An angel appeared with instructions for him to go to the desert (Acts 8:26), and by God's appointment he met the Ethiopian to whom he became the voice for God in preaching the word of truth.

Angels visited John, too. As he looked out upon the lonely seas from the Isle of Patmos and wondered why he was isolated from all but heaven, the angel of the apocalypse came to announce the message that formed the book of Revelation with its prophecies of the end time (Revelation 1:1–3).

An angel ministered in a somewhat similar way in an incident in Daniel's life. Chapter 5 describes a great feast ordered by Belshazzar in Babylon. It had been prepared ostensibly to show the glory of the kingdom, but in reality Belshazzar meant it to parade his own personal greatness. It was a feast for the thousands of his kingdom's greatest nobles. But on this occasion they desecrated the sacred vessels taken from the Temple at Jerusalem by using them for an ignoble purpose: They ate, drank and offered homage to idols of wood and stone, silver and gold. The god of materialism was in power. Suddenly the fingers of a man's hand appeared and traced on the wall a record of God's judgment on Babylon. "*Mene, Mene, Tekel, Upharsin,*" the hand wrote—"You have been weighed in the balances and been found wanting. Your kingdom is finished" (verses 25–27). It was one of God's angels sent to announce the impending judgment. Not only were the days of King Belshazzar numbered, but God was finished with him.

Later Daniel prayed for the people, "And he [Gabriel] informed me, and talked with me, and said, O Daniel, I am now come forth to give thee skill and understanding. . . . therefore, understand the matter, and consider the vision" (Daniel 9:22–23). In answer to Daniel's prayer, God gave him a panoramic view of the future "history" of the human race. It is my belief that the world is now possibly reaching the climax of those great visions that God gave Daniel.

The scene in the time of Belshazzar seems almost contemporary, those times and conditions resembling so closely what we see and hear today. It may even be that God is writing another story of impending judgment through the crises of the hour. He is telling men everywhere that unless they repent for their sins, their days like Belshazzar's are numbered and they are finished.

Let us conclude this study of the personal ministry of angels by noting some further incidents when God used angels to declare His plan to men.

At the beginning of the New Testament, Zacharias the priest saw the angel of the Lord, receiving from him the message that proclaimed the birth of John, who was to prepare the way for the promised Messiah. The angel (Gabriel in this instance, a special angelic minister of promise) encouraged Zacharias to believe the miracle surrounding the birth of John.

Later Gabriel appeared to the Virgin Mary, announcing to her the divinely conceived plan of the incarnation by which God's Son, Jesus Christ, should be conceived miraculously in her womb by the power of the Holy Spirit. Whatever Mary's questions may have been, they were answered by the angel's witness, "The Holy Ghost shall come upon thee, and the power of the Highest shall overshadow thee: therefore also that holy thing which shall be born of thee shall be called the Son of God" (Luke 1:35). Not only did Gabriel, that special angel of ministry and revelation, bring this message to Mary, but either he or another angel also confirmed to Joseph that he should take Mary as his wife, "For that which is conceived in her is of the Holy Ghost" (Matthew 1:20). He also told Joseph the plan of God that Jesus should "save his people from their sins" (Matthew 1:21).

The special angels of proclamation have faithfully bridged the centuries, carrying the message of God's will in times of oppression, discouragement and waning endurance. God's restoring servants, His heavenly messengers, have encouraged, sustained and lifted the spirits of many flagging saints; and they have changed many hopeless circumstances into bright prospect. Angels have ministered the message, "All is well," to satisfy fully the physical, material, emotional and spiritual needs of His people. They could testify, "The angel of the Lord came unto me."

CHAPTER 8

Angels Protect and Deliver Us

The enemies of Christ who attack us incessantly would often be thwarted if we could grasp God's assurance that His mighty angels are always nearby, ready to help. Tragically, most Christians have failed to accept this fact so frequently expressed in the Bible. I have noticed, though, that in my travels the closer I get to the frontiers of the Christian faith the more faith in angels I find among believers. Hundreds of stories document extraordinary divine intervention every year: God is using His angels as ministering spirits.

God's angels often protect His servants from potential enemies. Consider II Kings 6:14–17. The king of Syria had dispatched his army to Dothan, learning that Elisha the prophet was there. Upon dressing in the morning, the prophet's helper exclaimed excitedly to Elisha that the surrounding countryside bristled with armies and implements of war. Elisha assured him, "Don't be afraid! . . .

our army is bigger than theirs" (verse 16 Living Bible). Elisha then prayed that God would open the eyes of the young man to see the hosts of protective angels: as He did so, the young man "could see horses and chariots of fire everywhere on the hills surrounding the city." This passage has been one of the great assurances and comforts to me in my ministry.

The angels minister to God's servants in time of hardship and danger. We find another outstanding illustration of this in Acts 27:23-25. Paul on his way to Rome faced shipwreck with more than two hundred others on board. Speaking to the fear-ridden crew he said, "There stood by me this night the angel of God, whose I am, and whom I serve, Saying, Fear not, Paul, thou must be brought before Caesar; and lo, God hath given thee all them that sail with thee" (verses 23, 24).

Some believe strongly that each Christian may have his own guardian angel assigned to watch over him or her. This guardianship possibly begins in infancy, for Jesus said, "Take heed that ye despise not one of these little ones; for I say unto you that in heaven their angels do always behold the face of my Father, who is in heaven" (Matthew 18:10).

The most important characteristic of angels is not that they have power to exercise control over our lives, or that they are beautiful, but that they work on our behalf. They are motivated by an inexhaustible love for God and are jealous to see that the will of God in Jesus Christ is fulfilled in us.

David says of angels, "He who dwelleth in the secret place of the Most High shall abide under the shadow of the Almighty. . . . For he shall give his angels charge over thee, to keep thee in all thy ways. They shall bear thee up . . . lest thou dash thy foot against a stone" (Psalm 91:1, 11, 12).

My wife, Ruth, tells of a strange incident in a Christian bookroom in Shanghai, China. She learned of it through her father, Dr. L. Nelson Bell, who served in the hospital in Tsingkiangpu, Kiangsu province. It was at this store that Dr. Bell bought his gospel portions and tracts to distribute among his patients.

The incident occurred in 1942, after the Japanese had won the war with China. One morning around nine o'clock, a Japanese truck stopped outside the bookroom. It was carrying five marines and was half-filled with books. The Christian Chinese shop assistant, who was alone at the time, realized with dismay that they had come to seize the stock. By nature timid, he felt this was more than he could endure.

Jumping from the truck, the marines made for the shop door; but before they could enter, a neatly dressed Chinese gentleman entered the shop ahead of them. Though the shop assistant knew practically all the Chinese customers who traded there, this man was a complete stranger. For some unknown reason the soldiers seemed unable to follow him, and loitered about, looking in at the four large windows, but not entering. For two hours they stood around, until after eleven, but never set foot inside the door. The stranger asked what the men wanted, and the Chinese shop assistant explained that the Japanese were seizing stock from many of the bookshops in the city, and now this store's turn had come. The two prayed together, the stranger encouraging him, and so the two hours passed. At last the soldiers climbed into their army truck and drove away. The stranger also left, without making a single purchase or even inquiring about any items in the shop.

Later that day the shop owner, Mr. Christopher Willis (whose Chinese name was Lee), returned. The shop assistant said to him, "Mr. Lee, do you believe in angels?"

"I do," said Mr. Willis.

"So do I, Mr. Lee." Could the stranger have been one of God's protecting angels? Dr. Bell always thought so.

Corrie ten Boom writes of a remarkable experience at the fearful Nazi Ravensbruck prison camp:

"Together we entered the terrifying building. At a table were women who took away all our possessions. Everyone had to undress completely and then go to a room where her hair was checked.

"I asked a woman who was busy checking the possessions of the new arrivals if I might use the toilet. She pointed to a door, and I discovered that the convenience was nothing more than a hole in the shower-room floor. Betsie stayed close beside me all the time. Suddenly I had an inspiration, 'Quick, take off your woolen underwear,' I whispered to her. I rolled it up with mine and laid the bundle in a corner with my little Bible. The spot was alive with cockroaches, but I didn't worry about that. I felt wonderfully relieved and happy. 'The Lord is busy answering our prayers, Betsie,' I whispered. 'We shall not have to make the sacrifice of all our clothes.'

"We hurried back to the row of women waiting to be undressed. A little later, after we had had our showers and put on our shirts and shabby dresses, I hid the roll of underwear and my Bible under my dress. It did bulge out obviously through my dress; but I prayed, 'Lord, cause now thine angels to surround me; and let them not be transparent today, for the guards must not see me.' I felt perfectly at ease. Calmly I passed the guards. Everyone was checked, from the front, the sides, the back. Not a bulge escaped the eyes of the guard. The woman just in front of me had hidden a woolen vest under her dress; it was taken from her. They let me pass, for they did not see me. Betsie, right behind me, was searched.

"But outside awaited another danger. On each side of the door were women who looked everyone over for a second time. They felt over the body of each one who passed. I knew they would not see me, for the angels were still surrounding me. I was not even surprised when they passed me by; but within me rose the jubilant cry, 'O Lord, if Thou dost so answer prayer, I can face even Ravensbruck unafraid.' "

Divine Surveillance

Every true believer in Christ should be encouraged and strengthened! Angels are watching; they mark your path. They superintend the events of your life and protect the interest of the Lord God, always working to promote His plans and to bring about His highest will for you. Angels are interested spectators and mark all you do, "for we are made a spectacle unto the world, and to angels, and to men" (I Corinthians 4:9). God assigns angelic powers to watch over you.

Hagar, Sarah's maid, had fled from the tents of Abraham. It is ironic that Abraham, after having scaled such glorious heights of faith, should have capitulated to his wife's conniving and scolding, and to the custom of that day, to father a child by Hagar. And it is ironic that Sarah his wife should have been so jealous that when their own son, Isaac, was born years later, she wanted to get rid of both Hagar and the earlier child, Ishmael. So Abraham's self-indulgence led to sorrow and he thrust Hagar out of his home.

Nonetheless, God sent His angel to minister to Hagar. "And the angel of the Lord found her by a fountain of water in the wilderness, by the fountain in the way to Shur" (Genesis 16:7). The angel spoke as an oracle of God, turning her mind away from the injury of the past with a promise of what she might expect if she placed her faith in God. This God is the God not only of Israel but the God of the Arab as well (for the Arabs come from the stock of Ishmael). The very name of her son, Ishmael, meaning "God hears," was a sustaining one. God promised that the seed of Ishmael would multiply, and that his destiny would be great on the earth as he now undertook the restless pilgrimage that was to characterize his descendants. The angel of the Lord revealed himself as the protector of Hagar and Ishmael. Hagar in awe exclaimed, "Thou God seest me" (Genesis 16:13), or as may be better translated, "I have seen Thou who seest all and who sees me."

Psalm 34:7 underscores the teaching that angels protect and deliver us, "The angel of the Lord encampeth round about those who fear him, and delivereth them." We also find this idea reflected in one of Charles Wesley's songs:

> Angels, where ere we go,
> Attend our steps whate'er betide.
> With watchful care their charge attend,
> And evil turn aside.

The great majority of Christians can recall some incident in which their lives, in times of critical danger, have been miraculously preserved

—an almost plane crash, a near car wreck, a fierce temptation. Though they may have seen no angels, their presence could explain why tragedy was averted. We should always be grateful for the goodness of God, who uses these wonderful friends called angels to protect us. Evidence from Scripture as well as personal experience confirms to us that individual guardian, guiding angels attend at least some of our ways and hover protectively over our lives.

The Scriptures are full of dramatic evidences of the protective care of angels in their earthly service to the people of God. Paul admonished Christians to put on all the armor of God that they may stand firmly in the face of evil (Ephesians 6:10–12). Our struggle is not against flesh and blood (physical powers alone), but against the spiritual (superhuman) forces of wickedness in heavenly spheres. Satan, the prince of the power of the air, promotes a "religion" but not true faith; he promotes false prophets. So the powers of light and darkness are locked in intense conflict. Thank God for the angelic forces that fight off the works of darkness. Angels never minister selfishly; they serve so that all glory may be given to God as believers are strengthened. A classic example of the protective agency of angels is found in Acts 12:5–11.

As the scene opened, Peter lay bound in prison awaiting execution. James, the brother of John, had already been killed, and there was little reason to suppose that Peter would escape the exe-

cutioner's axe either. The magistrates intended
to put him to death as a favor to those who op-
posed the gospel and the works of God. Surely
the believers had prayed for James, but God had
chosen to deliver him through death. Now the
church was praying for Peter.

As he lay sleeping an angel appeared, not de-
terred by such things as doors or iron bars. The
angel came into the prison cell, shook Peter
awake and told him to prepare to escape. As a
light shone in the prison the chains fell off Peter,
and having dressed, he followed the angel out.
Doors supernaturally opened because Peter could
not pass through locked doors as the angel had.
What a mighty deliverance God achieved through
His angel!

Many experiences in both Old and New Testaments grew out of the imprisonment of God's
saints, calling either for God to deliver directly,
or to intervene through angels acting in His
name. Many today who are captive in the chains
of depression can take courage to believe in the
prospect of deliverance. God has no favorites and
declares that angels will minister to all the heirs
of faith. If we, the sons of God, would only realize
how close His ministering angels are, what calm
assurance we could have in facing the cataclysms
of life. While we do not place our faith directly in
angels, we should place it in the God who rules
the angels; then we can have peace.

Hebrews 11 contains a long list of men and
women of faith. For most of them God performed

miracles, delivering them from disease, calamity, accidents and even death. Someone has called this chapter, "God's Hall of Fame." Angels helped these great men and women to subdue kingdoms, obtain promises, stop the mouths of lions, quench the violence of fire, escape the edge of the sword, and when they were weak, stand with the help of angels to defeat entire armies.

But the tempo changes in verse 35, with the opening words, "and others were tortured, not accepting deliverance." Those now mentioned were of equal faith and courage: they had to endure the trial of cruel mockings and scourgings. They suffered bonds and imprisonment. They were stoned, they were sawn asunder, they were slain with the sword. They wandered about in goatskins, being destitute, afflicted and tormented. Time after time they must have called on God to send His mighty angels to help. No delivering angel came. They suffered and endured almost as though there were no God.

Why? We find a clue when our Lord faced Calvary as He prayed, "If it be possible let this cup pass from me" (Matthew 26:39); but then He added, "nevertheless not my will, but thine, be done" (Luke 22:42). In the sufferings and death of these great saints not physically delivered, God had a mysterious plan, and was performing His will. Knowing this, they suffered and died *by faith*. The latter part of Hebrews 11 indicates that those who received no visible help in answer to prayer will have a far greater heavenly reward because they endured by "faith" alone. But having died, they did enjoy the ministry of angels who then escorted their immortal souls to the throne of God. If the first part of Hebrews 11 is called "God's Hall of Fame," the second should be called, "God's Winners of the Medal of Honor."

Once when I was going through a dark period I prayed and prayed, but the heavens seemed to be brass. I felt as though God had disappeared and that I was all alone with my trial and burden. It was a dark night for my soul. I wrote my mother about the experience, and will never forget her reply: "Son, there are many times when God withdraws to test your faith. He wants you to trust Him in the darkness. Now, Son, reach up by faith in the fog and you will find that His hand will be there." In tears I knelt by my bed and experienced an overwhelming sense of God's presence. Whether or not we sense and feel the presence of the Holy Spirit or one of the holy angels, by faith we are certain God will never leave us nor forsake us.

CHAPTER 9

Angels — God's Agents in Judgment

The Bible says that throughout history angels have worked to carry out God's judgments, directing the destinies of nations disobedient to God. For example, God used angels in scattering the people of Israel because of their sins. He also used angels in bringing judgment on Sodom and Gomorrah, and eventually on Babylon and Nineveh. Further, at "the end of the age" angels will execute judgment on those who have rejected God's love.

The writer of Hebrews speaks of angelic forces as executors of God's judgments: "Who maketh his angels spirits, and his ministers a flame of fire" (Hebrews 1:7). The flaming fire suggests how awful are the judgments of God and how burning is the power of the angels who carry out God's decisions. Angels administer judgment in accord with God's principles of righteousness.

Unknown to men they have undoubtedly in the

past helped destroy evil systems like Nazism, because those governments came to the place where God could no longer withhold His hand. These same angels will carry out fearful judgments in the future, some of which the book of Revelation vividly describes.

We often get false notions about angels from plays given by Sunday school children at Christmas. It is true that angels are ministering spirits sent to help the heirs of salvation. But just as they fulfill God's will in salvation for believers in Jesus Christ, so they are also "avengers" who use their great power to fulfill God's will in judgment. God has empowered them to separate the sheep from the goats, the wheat from the chaff, and one of them will blow the trumpet that announces impending judgment when God summons the nations to stand before Him in the last great judgment.

Angels Warn of Judgment

In the case of Sodom and Gomorrah, there was no way judgment could be averted. Their wickedness had become too great. God had judged them; they had to be destroyed. But before God sends judgment, He warns. In this case, He used angels to point out to Abraham the approaching doom of Sodom and Gomorrah for their wickedness (Genesis 18). Abraham, whose nephew, Lot, and his family lived among these wicked people, began to plead with God to spare the two cities. Abraham asked God if He would avert judgment if fifty righteous people lived in Sodom. God told Abraham He would not destroy the city if there were fifty such people. Then Abraham asked for a stay of execution if there were only forty-five righteous people. God agreed. Then Abraham asked for deliverance if there were thirty righteous people. God agreed. Abraham then asked for twenty; then for ten. God agreed to withhold judgment if as many as ten righteous people could be found in Sodom. But not even ten such people lived there. Notice that God answered Abraham every time he asked. And He did not leave off answering until Abraham left off asking.

After this, God ordered the angelic ministers of judgment to rain destruction on these two wicked cities and all their inhabitants. Prior to the destruction of the cities, however, two unidentified heavenly messengers visited Sodom to warn Lot and his family to flee from the wrath about to come. So evil were the inhabitants of Sodom that they wanted to molest the angels physically. The angels blinded them and prevented them from carrying out their iniquitous conduct. In his book, *All About Angels,* C. Leslie Miller states, "It is significant that although Lot, Abraham's nephew, had drifted far from the holy standards of his uncle and had sought the companionship and material benefits of an unholy alliance, yet the angels of the Lord were there to spare his life and assist him in avoiding the consequences of his own poor judgment."

Thus, we see something of the mercy, grace and love of God toward even those who profess His name and try sincerely to live a God-honoring life in the midst of the most difficult circumstances.

The Angel Who Destroyed the Assyrian Army

In II Kings 19, Scripture dramatically underscores God's use of angels to execute His judgments. King Hezekiah had received a letter from the commander of the Assyrian forces and immediately sought God's counsel. God gave Isaiah the answer, saying that not one Assyrian arrow would be fired into the city. He promised to defend Jerusalem on that occasion for David's sake. Dramatically, that night, just one angel struck the Assyrian encampment and one hundred eighty-five thousand soldiers were found dead on the field of battle the next morning (verse 35).

The Angel Who Almost Destroyed Jerusalem

Nowhere in the Old Testament is there a more significant use of angelic power in judgment against God's own people than when David defied God's command by numbering Israel. God sent a pestilence among the Israelites and 70,000 died.

He also sent a single angel to destroy the city of Jerusalem. David "saw the angel of the Lord stand between the earth and the heaven, having a drawn sword in his hand stretched out over Jerusalem" (I Chronicles 21:16).

When David pleaded for mercy, the angel told him to set up an altar on the threshing floor of Ornan the Jebusite. God then accepted David's sacrifice there and said to the destroying angel, "It is enough: stay now thine hand" (II Samuel 24:16). The Scripture significantly says that the same angel had already slain the 70,000 men (verse 17). Indeed angels are God's agents in judgment.

New Testament history also records incidents where avenging angels judged the unrighteous acts of men and nations.

The Angel Who Smote Herod Agrippa

We have already referred to the case of Herod. Dressed in his royal apparel, he appeared before the people to make a speech. When he finished the people shouted, "It is the voice of a god, and not of a man" (Acts 12:22). Instead of disclaiming any such thing Herod delighted in the impact he had made. God's response to this idolatrous act was prompt, and for Herod, disastrous. "Because he gave not God the glory," he "was eaten of worms, and gave up the ghost" (verse 23). "The angel of the Lord smote him."

The Angel Who Destroyed the Egyptian First Born

One fateful night in Egypt just before the Exodus, the destroying angel was about to sweep over the land with a visitation of death (Exodus 12:18–30). How deeply must anxiety have etched itself upon the hearts of the Israelites. Believing Jews had offered sacrifices and generously sprinkled the blood over doorposts and lintels of their homes. Then in accord with God's time schedule, judgment fell on Egypt as the dark and awesome moment of midnight arrived. The destroying angel (I Corinthians 10:10, Hebrews 11:28) was God's minister of judgment, leaving death in his wake. The first born of every unbelieving Egyptian or Israeli household died under the judgment of a holy God who, however, had respect for the blood.

Down through the centuries this heart-rending account has been the theme of Jews and Christians alike: "When I see the blood, I will pass over you." It has been the text of thousands of sermons by rabbis and Christian clergymen. It was not the quality of life of the people in the blood-sprinkled houses that counted. It was their faith, apart from works, that they showed by sprinkling the blood. God had respect for only one thing: the blood sprinkled by faith.

How fearful it is to have these mighty angels carry out the judgments of an all-powerful God.

The Angel Who Stopped Abraham

In Genesis 22, God, wanting to test the reality of Abraham's faith, told him to sacrifice his beloved "son of promise," Isaac. God said, "Abraham . . . take now thy son, thine only son Isaac, whom thou lovest, and get thee into the land of Moriah; and offer him there for a burnt offering upon one of the mountains which I will tell thee of" (Genesis 22:1–2). What great suffering must have haunted and hurt the heart of Abraham through the long night as he considered what this supreme sacrifice entailed. Nevertheless, with nothing to go on but God's Word, Abraham by sheer naked faith took fire, wood and his son, and set off to do God's bidding. The Bible records no greater act of faith.

Having prepared the altar, Abraham placed Isaac, bound hand and foot, on the altar; then, unsheathing his knife, he raised his face toward heaven in submission to the Father's will. As Abraham lifted the knife in the air to plunge it into the heart of Isaac, "the angel of the Lord called unto him out of heaven, and said, Abraham, Abraham . . . Lay not thine hand upon the lad, neither do thou any thing unto him; for now I know that thou fearest God, seeing thou hast

not withheld thy son, thine only son from me"
(Genesis 22:11–12).

The double use of the name always implies
the importance of the message about to be given.
When he heard his name called, faithful Abraham responded immediately, and God rewarded
him for his unqualified obedience. "Abraham
lifted up his eyes, and looked, and, behold, behind him a ram caught in a thicket by his horns:
and Abraham went and took the ram, and offered
him up for a burnt offering *in the stead of* his
son" (Genesis 22:13).

Many scholars believe, as I do, that the angel
here is a "theophany," an appearance of the Lord
Jesus Christ Himself. He assumed the role of an
angel and God showed the principle of substitu-
tionary atonement: God had demanded of Abraham the death of his son. The demand for the
burnt offering had to be met, and it was met. But
in the place of Isaac, God through an angel accepted the animal substitute. That same principle
applies to us. True judgment demands that we
die. And the judgment must be executed. But
Jesus Christ Himself was the substitute offering.
He died so that we do not have to die. He took
our place so that the words used here, "in the
stead of," can be wonderfully applied to every
person who trusts in Christ. He died "in the stead
of" all who believe on Him.

How could God have asked for a human sacrifice? How could He have asked Abraham to slay
Isaac when He had forbidden the killing of peo-

ple (Genesis 9:6)? Is not this inconsistent with the nature of God? He gives us the answer to these questions about judgment by death in the Epistle to the Romans. "He that spared not his own Son, but delivered him up for us all, how shall he not with him also freely give us all things?" (Romans 8:32.) God could ask Abraham to slay Isaac because God Himself was willing to let His own Son die. He was not asking Abraham to do anything more than He was willing to do with His only begotten Son.

Neither Abraham nor Isaac had to drink the cup God presented. Isaac did not die and Abraham did not slay him. But when we come to another cup in the Garden of Gethsemane, the picture is startlingly different. Jesus has now come; as the guiltless one for the guilty, as the sinless one for sinners He was willing to accept the condemnation of God for the world's guilt, identifying Himself with it through His own death on Calvary.

Neither man nor angel could ever understand what was implied in the "cup" Jesus took in the Garden of Gethsemane that was to lead to His awful suffering, condemnation and death (Mark 14:36, Luke 22:42). In the Garden as He wrestled over the cup He was to drink, no ministering angel could spare Him from it or alleviate His suffering. It was His and His alone. It settled down on the Savior as a cup of judgment. He accepted and took upon Himself as the righteous one bearing the guilt of the wicked. The angels would have helped Him in that hour, but Christ did not call for their help. This one who said No to angel help said, in effect, "I will die for the sins of men because I love them so much." And in dying He was forsaken by men, by angels, and by the Father who is of purer eyes than to look upon sin and who in His Son's atoning agony turned His face from Him. That is why Jesus cried from the cross, "My God, my God, why hast thou forsaken me?" (Matthew 27:46.) He died alone. Angels were ready to rescue Him, but He refused.

Angels and Those Who Reject Jesus

It is clear in Scripture that angels will be God's emissaries to carry out His judgment against those who deliberately reject Jesus Christ and the salvation God offers through Him. While all men are sinners by nature, choice and practice, yet it is their deliberate rejection of Jesus Christ as Savior and Lord that causes the judgment of eternal separation from God.

God has assigned angels at the end of the age to separate the sheep from the goats, the wheat from the tares, the saved from the lost. We are not called upon to obey the voice of angels. But we are to heed and obey the Word of God and the voice of God that calls upon us to be reconciled to Him by faith in Jesus Christ. If not, we will have to pay the penalty of unforgiven sin.

The angels will administer that penalty. They "shall cast them into the furnace of fire" (Matthew 13:50). I am constantly astounded that God's decrees and warnings are considered so lightly in our modern world—even among Christians.

Angels and Eternal Life

Every son of Adam's race is confronted with two ways of life: one, to eternal life; the other, to eternal death. We have seen how angels execute God's judgment on those who reject Jesus; the angels cast them into the furnace of fire. But there is a totally different judgment: It is the good and wonderful judgment unto everlasting life. God gives the angels a place in this too. He commissions them to escort each believer to heaven and to give him a royal welcome as he enters the eternal presence of God. Each of us who trust Christ will witness the rejoicing of angelic hosts around the throne of God.

In the story of the rich man and Lazarus (Luke 16), Jesus told of a beggar who died in the faith. He had never owned many of this world's goods, but he was rich in faith that counts for eternity. When he died he was "carried by the angels into Abraham's bosom." Here were angelic pallbearers who took his immortal spirit to the place of glory where he was to be eternally with God—the place the Bible calls "heaven."

Another beautiful account of this kind comes from the life of the martyr Stephen (Acts 6:8–7:60). The "council, looking stedfastly on him, saw his face as it had been the face of an angel." Then Stephen in a powerful sermon declared that even unbelievers "received the law by the disposition of angels, and have not kept it" (Acts 7:53). When he had finished his discourse Stephen saw the glory of God and Jesus at the Father's right hand. Immediately his enemies stoned him to death and he was received into heaven. Even as the angels escorted Lazarus when he died, so we can assume that they escorted Stephen; and so they will escort us when by death we are summoned into the presence of Christ. We can well imagine what Stephen's abundant entrance to heaven was like as the anthems of the heavenly host were sung in rejoicing that the first Christian martyr had come home to receive a glorious welcome and to gain the crown of a martyr.

CHAPTER 10

Angels and the Gospel

While God has delegated angels to make special pronouncements for Him, He has not given them the privilege of proclaiming the gospel message. Why this is so, Scripture does not say. Perhaps spirit-beings who have never experienced the effects of separation from fellowship with God because of sin would be unable to preach with understanding.

But notice what the writer says in "Holy, Holy Is What the Angels Sing":

Holy, Holy is what the angels sing,
And I expect to help them make the
  courts of heaven ring.
And when I sing redemption's story,
They will fold their wings,
For angels never felt the joy
  that our salvation brings.

Down through the ages man's heart has remained unchanged. Whatever the color of his skin, whatever cultural or ethnic background, he needs the gospel of Christ. But who has God ordained to bring that gospel to fallen men? Fallen angels cannot do it; they cannot even be saved from their own sins. Yet unfallen angels cannot preach the gospel either. Presumably they do not hear the gospel the way we do; in their purity they have escaped the effects of sin and are unable to comprehend what it means to be lost.

Rather, God has commanded the Church to preach. This great task is reserved to believers. God has no other means. Only man can speak salvation's experience to man.

God has, however, assigned angels to assist those who preach. Their assistance includes the use of miraculous and corroborating signs. Missionaries of the eighteenth and nineteenth centuries have reported many wonderful incidents where angels seemed to help them proclaim the gospel. My wife, whose parents were missionaries to China, can remember many instances in her life where angels must have intervened in the ministry of her father and his fellow missionaries.

At any rate, you and I have the privilege of conveying a message to men from God in heaven, a message that angels cannot speak. Think of that! The story is told of a question asked of God: "In the event that men fail to preach the gospel as you have commanded, what other plan have you in mind?" "I have no other plan," He said.

No angel can be an evangelist. No angel can pastor a church, although angels watch over particular churches. No angel can do counseling. No angel can enjoy sonship in Jesus or be partaker of the divine nature or become a joint heir with Jesus in His kingdom. You and I are a unique and royal priesthood in the universe, and we have privileges that even angels cannot experience.

The Angel and Zacharias

The birth of John the Baptist was dynamically connected with the "evangel" (a term meaning the gospel, the good news of God's salvation in Jesus Christ). His parents, Zacharias and Elizabeth, were both old, Elizabeth being beyond the age to bear children. She and her husband were descendants of Aaron and thus connected with the priesthood. Both walked blameless before the Lord and kept His commandments. They illustrate how God works through godly parents; not infrequently we find that some of His greatest servants have enjoyed the benefits of a godly home. John and Charles Wesley, founders of the Methodist Church, came from a godly home and were profoundly influenced by their mother. Adoniram Judson, the great missionary to India, came from a minister's home. Jonathan Edwards, pastor, evangelist, educator, in early America, was from a line of godly forebears.

When the angel appeared to Zacharias to announce the good news that Elizabeth would, despite her age, give birth to a son, his words were immersed in the evangel. He predicted John's ministry: "Many of the children of Israel shall he turn to the Lord their God" (Luke 1:16). Thus, we learn that no one should presume that any person is saved, not even one born to a believing home, who has believing forebears, and grows up in a believing church. Moreover John was "to make ready a people prepared for the Lord" (verse 17).

How great the message of the angel was and how seriously Zacharias regarded it can be seen from events some months later. Zacharias lost his ability to speak following the angel's visit; he did not regain it until the birth of John. But at that time his tongue was loosed and he was filled with the Holy Spirit. His thinking—during the long months while Elizabeth awaited the birth of the baby—now burst out in his first words, which reflect the angel's visit and concern for the evangel. Zacharias says, "Blessed be the Lord God of Israel; for he hath visited and redeemed his people, and hath raised up an horn of salvation for us in the house of his servant David." A moment later he added, "And thou, child, [that is, John] shalt . . . give knowledge of salvation unto his people by the remission of their sins, Through the tender mercy of our God; whereby the dayspring from on high hath visited us, To give light to them that sit in darkness and in the shadow of death, to guide our feet into the way of peace" (Luke 1:76–79).

Now that was really a message! And all of it

rises from the visit of the angel, who told Zacharias about God's intention for John. But notice especially that the angel came, not simply to announce the birth of John, but to make it clear that John was to live his life as the forerunner of the Messiah, and as one who would bring the knowledge of salvation and the remission of sins to his fellow Israelites.

The Angel and the Evangel in the Birth of Jesus

The announcement to Mary that she was to be the mother of Jesus was made by no ordinary angel. It was Gabriel, one of three angels whose names have been given us in Scripture, who made the announcement. And it was connected with the evangel. This was true both of the words Gabriel spoke and the words Mary spoke while she was pregnant and looking toward the birth of her son. The angel told Mary that Jesus would be the Son of the Highest, that He would inherit the throne of His father David, would reign over the house of Jacob forever, and would have an everlasting kingdom. This was something far different from anything promised anyone else in Scripture. It was not promised to Abraham, or David or Solomon. Only Jesus' name is connected with these promises, and all of them are inextricably connected with both personal and national salvation.

After Mary became pregnant she visited Elizabeth and sang one of the sweetest songs known to literature. In it she makes evident that she has grasped what the angel told her. And what he told her she describes as salvation and the remission of sins: "My spirit hath rejoiced in God my Saviour" (Luke 1:47). Here was the news that Mary herself needed a Savior, and had found Him. The very baby who was encased in her womb would one day offer Himself as a propitiation for her and for all men. And that baby in her womb was God Almighty who had humbled Himself in order to dwell among us in the flesh.

Indeed she cries out that God's "mercy is on them that fear him from generation to generation." What is this but the glorious evangel, gospel, that God was in Christ reconciling the world to himself? And this was the message Gabriel brought to Mary. He could not preach it himself, but he could bear witness to the gospel that was to be preached by Jesus Christ and His followers through all ages.

The Angel, the Evangel and Joseph

Joseph, the husband of Mary, was caught up in a seemingly abysmal situation. He was legally engaged to a girl who was pregnant. He knew he was not the father because they had not yet consummated their forthcoming marriage. Yet Mary was apparently guilty of adultery under Jewish law, unless Joseph was willing to believe her story that the Holy Spirit had come upon her, and that she had never engaged in sexual relations with a man. As the innocent party, Joseph was thinking seriously of putting Mary away according to the custom of that day. The Scripture says that "while he thought on these things" (Matthew 1:20), an angel appeared to him in a dream and told him the true story of the incarnation and the role of Mary. Responding, Joseph believed the angel. But the announcement contained more than the simple fact that Mary was innocent of any transgression and that Joseph was the chosen vessel of God in affording her protection in this extraordinary event.

The angel also told Joseph something that was to witness to the gospel. Though the angel could not preach to Joseph, he struck at the root of the matter when he proclaimed, "He shall save his people from their sins" (Matthew 1:21). Here was the gospel in all of its beauty, simplicity and purity. According to the witness of the angel, sins can be forgiven. There is someone who can forgive sins. This is Jesus the Christ. The Savior has a people about whom He is concerned and guarantees that their sins shall be forgiven. In the midst of the wonder of the incarnation we should not overlook the fact that the angel was here bearing witness to the "evangel," the gospel. Jesus was not coming simply as God. He was coming as Redeemer and Savior to make men right with His Father and to assure them of the gift of everlasting life.

Gabriel, the Evangel and Daniel

Long before the days of Zacharias, Elizabeth, Mary, Joseph and John the Baptist, the angel Gabriel had borne witness of the evangel to the prophet Daniel. He had done this in connection with the prophecy of the seventy weeks. Daniel was deep in prayer, confessing both his sin and that of his people. While he was praying Gabriel appeared to him. Notice again that Gabriel did not preach the word of salvation, but he bore eloquent testimony to it. He said that the seventy weeks were designed "to finish the transgression, to make an end of sins, and to make reconciliation for iniquity" (Daniel 9:24). Then he foretold the cutting off of the Messiah, an event that Isaiah 53 had prophesied and depicted so dramatically.

The Jews had had difficulty understanding the notion of a suffering Messiah, rather picturing Him as one who would come in power and glory to overthrow their enemies and to reign triumphantly over them. But Gabriel told Daniel that sin is a reality, and must be paid for. The Messiah will do this by being cut off; that is, He will die for the sins of men. Then the power of sin to separate us from God will end, and men will be reconciled to Him. We see that though Gabriel could not preach, he could prophesy! And how beautifully the prophecies of the Old Testament are linked together with the fulfillment in the New

Testament. How gracious God was to use His angels as agents to make it plain to all they visited in all ages that their business was to witness to the evangel.

The Angel, the Evangel and the Shepherds

Does it not seem mysterious that God brought the first message of the birth of Jesus to ordinary people rather than to princes and kings? In this instance, God spoke through His holy angel to the shepherds who were keeping sheep in the fields. This was a lowly occupation, so shepherds were not well educated. But Mary in her song, the Magnificat, tells us the true story: "He hath put down the mighty from their seats, and exalted them of low degree. He hath filled the hungry with good things, and the rich he hath sent empty away" (Luke 1:52, 53). What a word for our generation!

What was the message of the angel to the shepherds? First, he told them not to be afraid. Over and over again the presence of angels was frightening to those to whom they came. But unless they came in judgment, the angels spoke a word of reassurance. They calmed the people to whom they came. This tells us that the appearance of an angel is awe-inspiring, something about them awakening fear in the human heart. They represent a presence that has greatness and sends a chill down the spine. But when the angel had quieted the fears of the shepherds, he brought this message, one forever to be connected with the evangel:

"For behold I bring you good tidings of great joy, which shall be to all people. For unto you is born this day in the city of David a Saviour, which is Christ the Lord" (Luke 2:10, 11). I could preach a dozen sermons on those two verses for they contain so many important theological themes. But note once more that the angel does not preach the gospel. Rather, he witnesses to it and demonstrates again the overwhelming concern angels have for it.

What did the angel say? First, he brought good tidings, not bad ones. The shepherds already knew the bad news—the human race had sinned and was lost. But the angel had come to tell them that God was doing something about their lostness. And he pointed out that the good news was not simply for the people of one nation, but for the whole world. Isaiah said, "The God of the whole earth shall he be called" (Isaiah 54:5). Jonah learned the same truth when he was sent to preach repentance to the people of Nineveh. The angel told the shepherds that the good tidings were for all people.

The good tidings were that the Savior had come. They needed somebody who could bring them back into fellowship with God, because the blood of bulls and goats could not do this in any permanent way. But the blood of the Savior could. The angel message was that God had come, redemption was possible, the Lord had visited His people with salvation. What a testimony to the evangel this was. And it was further validated when the angel who was accompanied by "a multitude of the heavenly host" began to chant or sing, "Glory to God in the highest, and on earth peace, good will toward men." Where could there be sweeter music? What hymn writer could match those words?

Angels and the Evangel in the Book of Acts

We might call two wonderful instances "case studies" of how angels see to it that unbelievers hear the gospel, respond to it and become saved. It shows again the concern of angels for the evangel and the steps they take to implement it.

The first case is that of the Ethiopian nobleman, a man of great authority. While reading the Old Testament Scriptures, he came to Isaiah and, unable to understand what the prophet meant, needed someone to interpret the Scripture to him. An angel knew of this situation. But the angel did not and could not do what the Ethiopian needed. He could not preach the gospel. But he could assist the Ethiopian eunuch by sending someone to him who could.

So the Scripture tells us that the angel spoke to Philip and specifically instructed him to go "toward the south unto the way that goeth down from Jerusalem unto Gaza, which is desert" (Acts 8:26). Philip obeyed the angel and approached

133

the chariot. Then he interpreted the Scripture for him and led him to a saving knowledge of Jesus Christ. After Philip had baptized the Ethiopian, the Spirit of the Lord caught him up and took him away. And the Ethiopian went on his way rejoicing. If the angel had been unconcerned about the evangel he would not have sent Philip to preach the gospel to this interested inquirer.

The second instance has to do with Peter and the conversion of Cornelius. In this case the situation is reversed. The angel had told Philip what to do so the Ethiopian could be saved. In this case he did not tell Peter what to do, but rather ordered Cornelius to send for Peter, who would then tell him the story of the gospel so he could be saved. Would it not have been much easier for the angel to have preached the gospel to Cornelius than to have had him send for Peter? After all, Peter was not a willing witness. He had the notion that it was wrong to preach the gospel for the salvation of Gentiles. Cornelius, however, followed the word of the angel and sent for Peter. Then God had to appear in a dream and convince Peter that it was all right for him to witness to a Gentile. Peter finally went and Cornelius was wonderfully saved. But it was done through the auspices of the angel who was deeply concerned with the evangel, and for the salvation of this Roman soldier.

One other story in the Acts of the Apostles is somewhat different, though no less worthy of consideration. It has to do with Paul on his way to Rome. He was shipwrecked en route. But while it appeared that the ship would sink with all hands lost, an angel of the Lord appeared to Paul at night. He told those aboard the ship that they would all be saved. Then he said something that illuminates the concern of angels for the salvation of men and the witness of Christians to the unsaved. "Fear not, Paul; thou must be brought before Caesar" (Acts 27:24). Here we see that same principle. The angel could not witness to Caesar, but Paul could. And God in His providence was sending him to Rome for precisely this purpose. If Paul had not fully known the will of God before, it was clear at this moment. God intended that Caesar should hear the gospel. And the angel, by bringing the message, revealed his own interest in the evangel.

The Sound of Angel Voices

The keynote of evangelism is couched in the heavenly proclamation I have mentioned, "Unto you is born this day . . . a Saviour which is Christ the Lord." And the task of world evangelization will be completed by men and women whom the Holy Spirit uses. But wherever and whenever we see the gospel working in its power to transform, there is a possibility that in some ways angels may be involved. This is a mystery that we will never quite understand until we get to heaven.

It is not unreasonable to ask, "What did the angel voices sound like?" And "What did they say when they spoke?" Angels seemed to communicate terse commands. Very often the angel messengers urged haste, and this is understandable since they were communicating a directive from God. Dr. Miller points out that the contemporary expression, "Hurry up," would fit most angel commands. The words," Get up," were sometimes literally used. The angel said to Peter, "Rise quickly." The angel said to Gideon, "Arise and go in this thy might." The angel said to Joseph, "Go quickly," and to Philip, "Arise and go."

In the same way any evangelistic ministry sounds the note of urgency concerning the gospel. We have no time to waste because we can never reclaim this moment. We may never have a second chance to witness if we neglect the first.

We can illustrate this from the sinking of the *Titanic*. The greatest ship of its day, weighing 46,000 tons, it was considered unsinkable. But on the night of April 14, 1912, while coursing through the ocean at 22 knots, it struck an iceberg. Because it carried only half as many life jackets as passengers, when it sank 1,513 people drowned.

One passenger, John Harper, was on his way to preach at Moody Church in Chicago. Trying to stay afloat in the ocean he drifted toward a young man holding onto a plank. Harper asked, "Young man, are you saved?" The man said, "No." A wave separated them. After a few minutes they drifted within speaking distance of each other, and again Harper called to him, "Have you made your peace with God?" The young man said, "Not yet." A wave overwhelmed John Harper and he was seen no more, but the words, "Are you saved?" kept ringing in the young man's ears.

Two weeks later a youth stood up in a Christian Endeavor meeting in New York, told his story and said, "I am John Harper's last convert."

CHAPTER 11

Angel Ministries in the Life of Jesus

It would take an entire book to spell out in detail how the life of Jesus was intertwined with the attending ministry of angels. Before He was here they followed His orders. And since He ascended into heaven they have worshiped Him before the throne of God as the Lamb slain for our salvation.

To prepare for the coming of Jesus an angel appeared to Zacharias to inform him that his wife would be the mother of John the Baptist (Luke 1:13). Gabriel, one of the mighty angels of God, announced to Mary that she would give birth to the Messiah. An angel and a multitude of the heavenly host spread the good news of Jesus' coming to the shepherds in the field (Luke 2:9). These angelic incidents preceded and accompanied His birth, but when Jesus began His public ministry angels were intimately involved in His life as well.

Perhaps the most difficult period in the life of Jesus before His crucifixion was His temptation by the devil in the wilderness. After He had fasted forty days and nights, Satan tried to break Him down. In Christ's weakened human condition, Satan began his attack, seeing this as his greatest opportunity to defeat the program of God in the world since his victory in the Garden of Eden. He was out to shipwreck the hope of the human race. Wishing to prevent the salvation of sinners, he struck at the moment when Christ's physical weakness made Him most susceptible to temptation. Satan always directs his sharpest attack at his victim's weakest point. He knows where the Achilles' heel may be and he does not fail to strike at the opportune time.

Three times Satan attempted to defeat Jesus. Three times Jesus quoted Scripture, and three times Satan went down to defeat. Then the Bible declares that "he [Satan] departed from him [Jesus] for a season" (Luke 4:13). It was at this point that angels came to His assistance—not to help Him resist Satan as they help us, for He did that by Himself, but to help Him after the battle was won. The angels "ministered" to Jesus. The Greek word *diakoneo* says it well, for they served Him as a deacon would serve. "Behold, angels came and ministered unto him" (Matthew 4:11). Angelic ambassadors supported, strengthened and sustained Him in that trying hour. From that moment on our Lord Jesus Christ, who was in all points tempted as we are, could sympathize and help Christian believers for the ages to come, and lead them to victory in their hour of temptation.

The Angel with Jesus in the Garden of Gethsemane

The night before His crucifixion Jesus was in the Garden of Gethsemane. Only a short time later He was to be seized by the soldiers, betrayed by Judas Iscariot, set before the rulers, beaten and at last crucified. Before He was hung on the cross He went through the terrible agony in the Garden which made Him sweat, as it were, drops of blood. It was in this situation that the Son of man needed inner strength to face what no other being in heaven, hell or earth had ever known. In fact, He was to face what no created being could have faced and gone through in victory. He was about to take upon Himself the sins of men. He was to become sin for us.

Jesus had taken Peter, James and John with Him to the Garden. They could have provided Him with reinforcement and encouragement, but instead they fell asleep. The Son of man was all alone. He prayed, "Father, if thou be willing, remove this cup from me: nevertheless not my will, but thine, be done" (Luke 22:42). Then it was at that crucial moment that the angel came to assist Him, "strengthening Him." The Greek word for strengthening is *eniskuo*, which means to make

strong inwardly. Where the disciples of the Lord
Jesus had failed to share His agony, as they slept
the angel came to help.

Angels Waiting at the Cross

The tragedy of sin reached its crescendo when
God in Christ became sin. At this point He was
offering Himself as the sacrifice required by the
justice of God if man was to be redeemed. At this
moment Satan was ready to try his master stroke.
If he could get Christ to come down from the
cross, and if Christ allowed the mockery of the
crowd to shame or anger Him, then the plan of
salvation would be jeopardized. Again and again
they shouted, "If thou be the Son of God, come
down from the cross" (Matthew 27:40). He knew
He could come down if He chose; He knew He
could get help from more than twelve legions of
angels who hovered about with drawn swords.

Yet for our salvation He stayed there. The
angels would have come to the cross to rescue the
King of kings, but because of His love for the
human race and because He knew it was only
through His death that they could be saved, He
refused to call for their help. The angels were
under orders not to intervene at this terrible, holy
moment. Even the angels could not minister to the
Son of God at Calvary. He died alone in order to
take the full death penalty you and I deserved.

We can never plumb the depths of sin, or sense

141

how terrible human sin is, until we go to the cross and see that it was "sin" that caused the Son of God to be crucified. The ravages of war, the tragedy of suicide, the agony of the poverty-stricken, the suffering and irony of the rejected of our society, the blood of the accident victim, the terror of rape and mug victims of our generation—these all speak as with a single voice of the degradation that besets the human race at this hour. But no sin has been committed in past history, nor is any being committed in the world today that can compare with the full cup of the universe's sin that brought Jesus to the cross. The question hurled toward heaven throughout the ages has been, "Who is He and why does He die?" The answer comes back, This is my only begotten Son, dying not only for your sins but for the sins of the whole world. To you sin may be a small thing; to God it is a great and awful thing. It is the second largest thing in the world; only the love of God is greater.

When we comprehend the great price God was willing to pay for the redemption of man, we only then begin to see that something is horribly wrong with the human race. It must have a Savior, or it is doomed! Sin cost God His very best. Is it any wonder that the angels veiled their faces, that they were silent in their consternation as they witnessed the outworking of God's plan? How inconceivable it must have seemed to them, when they considered the fearful depravity of sin, that Jesus should shoulder it all. But they were soon to unveil their faces and offer their praises again. A light was kindled that day at Calvary. The cross blazed with the glory of God as the most terrible darkness was shattered by the light of salvation. Satan's depraved legions were defeated and they could no longer keep all men in darkness and defeat.

The Angels at the Resurrection

On the third day after His death the Scripture says, "And behold there was a great earthquake; for the angel of the Lord descended from heaven, and came and rolled back the stone from the door, and sat upon it. His countenance was like lightning, and his raiment white as snow: And for fear of him the keepers did shake, and became as dead men" (Matthew 28:2–4).

Though some Bible students have tried to estimate how much this stone weighed, we need not speculate because Jesus could have come out of that tomb whether the stone was there or not. The Bible mentions it so that generations to come can know something of the tremendous miracle of resurrection that took place. I have often wondered what those guards must have thought when, against the brightness of the rising sun, they saw the angel rolling away the gigantic boulder with possibly the lightest touch of his finger! The guards, though heavily armed, were paralyzed with fear.

143

As Mary looked into the tomb she saw "two angels in white sitting, the one at the head, and the other at the feet, where the body of Jesus had lain" (John 20:11, 12). Then one of the angels who was sitting outside the tomb proclaimed the greatest message the world has ever heard: "He is not here, but is risen" (Luke 24:6). Those few words changed the history of the universe. Darkness and despair died; hope and anticipation were born in the hearts of men.

Angels and the Ascension of Jesus

We find the story of the ascension of Jesus in Acts 1. Verse 9 says, "And when he had spoken these things, while they beheld, he was taken up; and a cloud received him out of their sight." Jesus had been accompanied to earth by an angelic host. I believe that the word "cloud" suggests that angels had come to escort Him back to the right hand of God the Father.

The watching disciples were sad and despondent. Tears filled their eyes. But again two angels, looking like men and dressed in white raiment, appeared and said, "Ye men of Galilee, why stand ye gazing up into heaven? This same Jesus, which is taken up from you into heaven, shall so come in like manner as ye have seen him go into heaven" (Acts 1:11).

Thus, the angels escorted the resurrected Lord of glory back to be seated at the Father's right hand; then even the morning stars ascribed honor, glory and praise to Him as the Son of the Living God. On the other hand, some angels remained behind to assure those early disciples that they would always be near, ready to help God's people throughout the ages to come—until Christ returns in person with the angelic host.

CHAPTER 12

Angels in Prophecy

Angels have an important role in future events! Human history began at Eden where God planted a garden and made man for His eternal fellowship. Angels were there. They have never failed to attend the human scene. And they will continue on the scene throughout the succeeding ages till time runs into eternity.

Just as millions of angels participated in the dazzling show when the morning stars sang together at creation, so will the innumerable hosts of heaven help bring to pass God's prophetic declarations throughout time and into eternity.

When God decrees it, Satan (Lucifer) will be removed from the world of disorder so God can establish righteousness everywhere, and a true theocracy. Not until that event takes place will the human race know perfect peace on earth. Paul tells us in Romans 8 that the whole creation

groans and travails as it awaits the day of Christ's
victory.

The prophets spoke of a wonderful day when
God would lift the curse, when lion and lamb
would lie down together, and when nations would
learn war no more (Isaiah 2:4, 11:6). Angel
hosts will fullfill His royal decrees and oversee
God's purpose in the universe. Christ is coming
in great power, and all His holy angels will be
with Him. In Acts 1:10, 11 angels gave counsel
to the disciples after Jesus had ascended to
heaven. As we have already seen, when He had
left the Mount of Olives, angels appeared, saying,
"Ye men of Galilee, why stand ye gazing up into
heaven? This same Jesus . . . shall so come in
like manner as ye have seen him go into heaven"
(Acts 1:11). Angels encouraged those downcast
believers who had seen Jesus Christ disappear from
their view into a cloud. After this, angels figure
prominently in the prophetic plan of God that
continued on into the future events of Bible
prophecy.

In every age, the true believers have asked,
"Will this conflict of the ages ever end?" Each
period of history seemingly has its own trials and
convulsions. Each generation seems to have to
"fight it out." Behind it all is the unseen struggle
of the ages. We thought that modern technology
would solve many of the great problems of the
human race. In some ways it has, by eliminating
the fear of diseases like polio and smallpox. But
it has also given us Frankenstein weapons of de-

struction. Poverty, greed, lust, war and death are still with us. This is the same war that began mysteriously in the heart of Lucifer. The title of A. C. Gaebelein's book, *Hopeless Yet There Is Hope,* expresses our position today. It seems that our world is on a suicidal course; but God has other plans. Light shines at the end of the tunnel. Someday Satan and his demons will go down in defeat. The Bible declares that righteousness will eventually triumph, Utopia will come to earth, the kingdom of God will ultimately prevail. In bringing all this about angels will have a prominent part.

A little girl heard a clock strike thirteen times. Breathlessly she ran to her mother and said, "Mother, it's later than it's ever been before." Almost everyone throughout the world will agree. It's later than it's ever been before. The human race is rushing madly toward some sort of climax. And the Bible accurately predicts what that climax is! A new world is coming. Through modern technology and scientific achievement we are catching glimpses of what that new world is. If it were not for depraved human nature, man could achieve it himself. But man's rebellion against God has always been his stumbling block. The penalty for man's rebellion is death. The best leaders and the best brains have many times been stopped by death. The Bible teaches that "it is appointed unto men once to die" (Hebrews 9:27). Today the world longs for a leader such as Abraham Lincoln —but death took him from us.

God will use the angels to merge time into eternity, creating a new kind of life for every creature. Even today's intellectual world speaks of a point when time will be no more. Most scientists agree that the clock of time is running out. Ecologically, medically, scientifically, morally, time is running out. Even the sun is gradually cooling. In almost every direction we look, man's time on earth seems to be running out. Self-destruction is overtaking us as a human race.

Will man destroy himself? No! God has another plan!

Since the beginning of time, man has been interested in what lies beyond the short span of life. Modern man is turning to the occult, Eastern mysticism, palm readers and every other kind of help available to tell him about the future. Strangely, only a minority turn to the Bible, the only book that accurately foretells the future. The Bible teaches that Jesus Christ is coming back again with His holy angels. It refers to His coming as the day of visitation (Isaiah 10:3), the evil day (Ecclesiastes 12:1), a day of wrath (Romans 2:5), and the judgment of the great day (Jude 6), with many other references both direct and indirect. The Age of Utopia will be preceded by unparalleled events of suffering for the human race—totalitarianism, poverty, disease, earthquakes, moral collapse, war—until men's hearts will fail them for fear.

Luke 21 says there will be "wars and commotions . . . Nation shall rise against nation, and kingdom against kingdom: And great earthquakes shall be in divers places, and famines, and pestilences; and fearful sights and great signs shall there be from heaven" (verses 9–11).

Believing Christians and believing Jews alike will be persecuted. Men will deliver "you up to the synagogues, and into prisons, being brought before kings and rulers for my name's sake. . . . And ye shall be betrayed both by parents, and brethren, and kinsfolks, and friends; and some of you shall they cause to be put to death. And ye shall be hated of all men for my name's sake. . . . And when ye shall see Jerusalem compassed with armies, then know that the desolation thereof is nigh. . . . For these be the days of vengeance [upon all the human race] that all things which are written may be fulfilled. . . . And there shall be signs in the sun, and in the moon, and in the stars; and upon the earth distress of nations, with perplexity; the sea and the waves roaring; men's hearts failing them for fear, and for looking after those things which are coming on the earth: for the powers of heaven shall be shaken" (verses 12–26).

Jesus continued in verse 27, "And then shall they see the Son of man coming in a cloud with power and great glory."

Even as in the beginning of time angelic forces waged war in heaven (Revelation 12:7–9), so in the very last days angels will wage still another war; Satan will make his last stand. As the time draws near he intensifies his activities.

But it will be a victorious day for the universe, and especially planet earth, when the devil and his angels are thrown into the lake of fire, never again to tempt and destroy man. To the angels God has assigned this task, and Scripture assures us that they will be victorious (Matthew 13:41, 42).

Angels Will Gather God's Elect

Linked to this idea Jesus says that "When the Son of man shall come in his glory, and all the holy angels with him, then shall he sit upon the throne of his glory" (Matthew 25:31). In other words, when Jesus returns, He will be accompanied by the hosts of heaven. The holy angels will be with Him! As He says in Matthew 13:41– 42, "The Son of man shall send forth his angels, and they shall gather out of his kingdom all things that offend, and them which do iniquity· And shall cast them into a furnace of fire: there shall be wailing and gnashing of teeth."

Earlier in this same chapter, Jesus has related a significant little story commonly called the Parable of the Tares and Wheat (Matthew 13:24–30, 36–43). Both had been allowed to grow together until the harvest, but then the reapers were to gather them up in bundles. The tares were to be burned: the wheat gathered. We often wonder why God permits so much sin in the world, why He withholds His right arm of judgment. Why doesn't

God put an end to sin now? We can give an answer from this text where Jesus said, "Let both grow together," the evil with the good (verse 30). If we were to try to wipe all evil from the face of the earth, who could count on justice? Pure justice does not exist here, because everyone is guilty, including the judges who sit in judgment. They are guilty of sin. Man must do his best in meting out justice, but his best is not complete justice. To angels will be delegated the ministry of separating the good from the bad, discerning even attitudes. God's judgment will be so pure that even those that are condemned will bow their knee and confess, "Thou art just." As someone has said, "When I die I do not want justice—I want mercy!" That mercy has been provided by the Lord Jesus Christ.

So angels will not only accompany Christ when He returns, but will be assigned the responsibility of gathering out of His kingdom all things that offend and work iniquity, that they might be judged (Matthew 13:47–50).

It boggles the mind to try to imagine the kind of earth this is going to be when God eliminates the devil and sin. Our minds are staggered at the thought of "Christ on the throne." The great southward-moving Sahara Desert of Africa will bloom and blossom. Mankind will be able to grow new foods; land that today is useless will grow twelve crops a year. The urge in man's heart toward immorality will have vanished. In that day the great drive in man will be a thirst for righteousness. It takes a great deal of faith in these days of despondency to believe this, but it is the clear teaching of the Bible. Without this hope of the future I do not know what modern man does, except turn to drugs and alcohol.

Today we have the choice of whether or not to receive the ministry of angels. In choosing to follow Jesus Christ we also choose the protective watch and care of the angels of heaven. In the time of the Second Coming, we will no longer be afforded the privilege of choice. If we delay now, it will be too late, and we forfeit forever the gracious ministry of angels and the promise of salvation to eternal life.

Angels in Our Future

Dr. Miller asks the question, "What does the future hold for this weary old world? . . . for the physical earth? The answers to such questions are not to be found in astrology or necromancy but in the divinely inspired Word of God. And we may be certain that, as the passing of time fulfills the prophetic Scriptures, the holy angels will be deeply involved in the fulfillment." God will renovate the earth, order the New Jerusalem to descend from heaven, and give redeemed man a position above the angels—what a future!

Elijah was one of the greatest prophets, suddenly appearing on the scene in one of Israel's darkest hours (I Kings 17). He was a strong, suntanned son of the desert. At times he could be bold as a lion, and at times crushed with frustration. On one occasion he challenged the prophets of the heathen god Baal to a duel to see who was the true God (I Kings 18:19). When the prophets of Baal could get no answer from their false god, and Elijah's God answered by fire, Queen Jezebel, unable to accept the prophet's verdict, determined to take his life and pursued him with her chariot for many miles. Elijah, weary from his flight and desperately hungry, lay down under a juniper tree to rest. Feeling extremely sorry for himself, he went to sleep, to be wakened by an angel's touch. Then food was set before him to eat, and the angel said, "Arise, eat."

"And he looked, and, behold, there was a cake baken on the coals, and a [jar] of water at his head. And he did eat and drink, and laid him down again. And the angel of the Lord came again the second time, and touched him, and said, Arise and eat: because the journey is too great for thee. And he arose, and did eat and drink, and went in the strength of that meat forty days and forty nights unto Horeb the mount of God" (I Kings 19:6-8).

God did not let his faithful prophet down. He provided just what he needed physically, psychologically and spiritually. Many of us despair of coping with the pressures of our lives, but if we are living Spirit filled and Spirit-directed lives, we can claim God's promises. The prophetic Scriptures give us "hope." Without Scripture's plan of God for the future and the hope it brings, I do not know what the average thinking person does. Certainly a person will not find the answer by wringing his hands, or by committing suicide, or by turning to the occult. We find the answer to the future in Holy Scripture. It is summed up in the person of Jesus Christ. God has centered all our hopes and dreams on Him. He is the Commander in Chief of these angelic armies that will accompany Him on His return.

Angel Authority

New Testament writers have reaffirmed the badge of authority given to angels to fulfill the prophetic dictates of God. "But unto the Son he saith, Thy throne, O God, is forever and ever" (Hebrews 1:8). The Apostle Peter emphasized this same truth when speaking of Christ, who was at the right hand of God, having gone into heaven after "angels and authorities and powers [had been] made subject unto him" (I Peter 3:22). The time is coming when the twenty-four elders of His angelic creation will fall down before the Lamb and sing their new song (Revelation 5:9–10). Thereafter, the holy angels will gather round the throne and join in a great testimony to the Lamb, expressing praise with such words as, "Worthy is the Lamb that was slain to receive power and riches and wisdom and might and honor and glory and blessing" (Revelation 5:12, ASV). While angels have tremendous authority, it is limited to doing only the will of God. They never deviate from God's message, never dilute His message, never change God's plan. Throughout the ages they have glorified only Him, never themselves.

The Bible teaches that the demons are dedicated to controlling this planet for their master, Satan. Even Jesus called him "the prince of this world" (John 12:31). He is the master-organizer and strategist. Many times throughout biblical history, and possibly even today, angels and demons engage in warfare. Many of the events of our times may very well be involved in this unseen struggle.

We are not left in doubt about who will ultimately triumph. Time after time Jesus has assured us that He and the angels would be victorious. "When the Son of man shall come in his glory, and all the holy angels with him, then shall he sit upon the throne of his glory" (Matthew 25:31). The Apostle Paul wrote, "The Lord Jesus shall be revealed from heaven with his mighty angels in flaming fire" . . . (II Thessalonians 1:7, 8).

Jesus also taught that "Whosoever shall confess me before men, him shall the Son of man also confess before the angels of God" (Luke 12:8). It is impossible to comprehend one's suffering of eternal loss when he learns that angels do not acknowledge him because he has been false in his claims to know Christ. But what a moment it is going to be for believers throughout all the ages, from every tribe, nation and tongue, when they are presented in the Court of Heaven. Scripture calls it, "the marriage supper of the Lamb" (Revelation 19:9). This is the great event when Jesus Christ is crowned King of kings and Lord of lords. Both believers of all ages and all the angelic hosts will join in bowing their knees and confessing that He is Lord.

The book of Revelation, from chapter four to nineteen, gives us a picture of judgments to befall the earth such as the world has never known. Angels will be involved in all of these judgments. But after these terrifying events, Christ will come with His holy angels to set up His Kingdom.

Whether the battle between the forces of Satan and the forces of God involve other planets and galaxies we do not know. But we do know that the earth is the scene of the conflict; however, it is a gigantic struggle that affects the entire universe. It is mind-boggling that you and I, with such a short period of time on this planet, play a part in this battle of the ages. It is almost incredible to us that supernatural beings from outer space are engaged in a struggle for this planet.

It all started in the Garden of Eden, a place located somewhere between the Tigris and the Euphrates rivers in the Middle East. It is significant that the nations prominent in early history are once again becoming prominent: Israel, Egypt, Syria, Persia, etc. In that Garden God gave a great promise, "And I will put enmity between thee and the woman, and between thy seed and her seed; it shall bruise thy head, and thou shalt bruise his heel" (Genesis 3:15). As we approach the end of the age, the head of Satan is being battered and bruised as the forces of God gain momentum. Under the command of God, Michael the archangel is now organizing his forces for the last battle—Armageddon. The last picture in the Bible is one of heaven.

Some time ago I was visiting the dining room of the United States Senate. As I was speaking to various people, Senator Magnuson of Washington called me to his table. He said, "Billy, we're having a discussion about pessimism and optimism. Are you a pessimist or an optimist?" I smiled and said, "I'm an optimist." He asked, "Why?" I said, "I've read the last page of the Bible."

The Bible speaks about a city whose builder and maker is God, where those who have been redeemed will be superior to angels. It speaks of "a pure river of water of life, clear as crystal, proceeding out of the throne of God and of the Lamb" (Revelation 22:1). It says, "And they shall see his face; and his name shall be in their foreheads. And there shall be no night there; and they need no candle, neither light of the sun; for the Lord God giveth them light: and they shall reign for ever and ever" (verses 4, 5).

The next verse has a thrilling last word to say about angels: "These sayings are faithful and true: and the Lord God of the holy prophets sent his angel to shew unto his servants the things which must shortly be done."

Christian and non-Christian alike should meditate on the seventh verse where God says, "Behold I come quickly: blessed is he that keepeth the sayings of the prophecy of this book."

CHAPTER 13

The Angels and Death

The angel who came to the garden where Jesus' body lay, rolled away the stone and permitted fresh air and morning light to fill His tomb. The sepulcher was no longer an empty vault or dreary dormitory; rather it was a life-affirming place that radiated the glory of the living God. No longer was it a dark prison but a transformed reminder of the celestial light that sweeps aside the shadows of death. Jesus' resurrection changed it.

An unknown poet has said of the tomb, " 'Tis now a cell where angels used to come and go with heavenly news." No words of men or angels can adequately describe the height and depth, the length and breadth of the glory to which the world awakened when Jesus came forth to life from the pall of death. As Charles Wesley says in a hymn:

> 'Tis mystery all! Th' Immortal dies!
> Who can explore His strange design?

In vain the first-born seraph tries
To sound the depths of love Divine!
'Tis mercy all! Let earth adore!
Let angel minds inquire no more.

In contrast to Jesus, we all still have to die. Yet just as an angel was involved in Christ's resurrection, so will angels help us in death. Only one thin veil separates our natural world from the spiritual world. That thin veil we call death. However, Christ both vanquished death and overcame the dark threats of the evil fallen angels. So now God surrounds death with the assurance of angelic help to bring pulsing life out of the darkness of that experience for believers. We inherit the kingdom of God.

Christians at Death

Death for the Christian cuts the cord that holds us captive in this present evil world so that angels may transport believers to their heavenly inheritance. Death is the fiery chariot, the gentle voice of the King, the invitation to nonstop passage into the banquet house of the world of glory.

In another connection I have already mentioned Lazarus, whom angels escorted to Abraham in heaven. This story has always been a tremendous comfort me as I think about death. I will actually be taken by angels into the presence of God. These ministering spirits who have helped me here so often will be with me in my last great battle on earth. Death is a battle, a profound crisis event. Paul calls it "the last enemy" (I Corinthians 15:26). While the sting of death has been removed by the work of Christ on the cross, and by His resurrection, yet the crossing of this valley still stimulates fear and mystery. However, angels will be there to help us. Could not the "rod and staff," which help us in the valley of the shadow of death (Psalm 23:4), be these holy angels?

We who have made our peace with God should be like the evangelist D. L. Moody. When he was aware that death was at hand, he said, "Earth recedes, heaven opens before me." It appeared as though he was dreaming. Then he said, "No, this is no dream . . . it is beautiful, it is like a trance. If this is death, it is sweet. There is no valley here. God is calling me, and I must go."

After having been given up for dead, Moody revived to indicate that God had permitted him to see beyond that thin veil separating the seen from the unseen world. He had been "within the gates, and beyond the portals," and had caught a glimpse of familiar faces whom he had "loved long since and lost awhile." Then he could remember when he had proclaimed so vociferously earlier in his ministry, "Some day you will read in the papers that D. L. Moody of East Northfield is dead. Don't you believe a word of it. At that moment I shall be more alive than I am now. I shall have gone up higher, that is all—out of this old clay tenement into a house that is immortal; a body that death cannot touch, that sin cannot taint, a body fashioned like unto His glorious body. . . . That which is born of the flesh may die. That which is born of the Spirit will live forever" (*The Life of Dwight L. Moody*, by W. R. Moody). If Moody were to witness to us now, he would surely tell us of the glowing experience that became his as the angelic hosts ushered him into the presence of the Lord.

Death is not natural, for man was created to live and not to die. It is the result of God's judgment because of man's sin and rebellion. Without God's grace through Christ, it is a gruesome spectacle. I have stood at the bedside of people dying without Christ; it was a terrible experience. I have stood at the bedside of those who were dying in Christ; it was a glorious experience. Charles Spurgeon said of the glory that attends the death of the redeemed, "If I may die as I have seen some die, I court the grand occasion. I would not wish to escape death by some by-road if I may sing as they sang. If I may have such hosannas and alleluias beaming in my eyes as I have seen as well as heard from them, it were a blessed thing to die."

Death is robbed of much of its terror for the true believer, but we still need God's protection as we take that last journey. At the moment of death the spirit departs from the body and moves through the atmosphere. But the Scripture teaches us that the devil lurks then. He is "the prince of the power of the air" (Ephesians 2:2). If the eyes of our understanding were opened, we would

probably see the air filled with demons, the enemies of Christ. If Satan could hinder the angel of
Daniel 10 for three weeks on his mission to earth,
we can imagine the opposition a Christian may
encounter at death.

But Christ on Calvary cleared a road through
Satan's kingdom. When Christ came to earth, He
had to pass through the devil's territory and open
up a beachhead here. That is one reason He was
accompanied by a host of angels when He came
(Luke 2:8–14). And this is why holy angels will
accompany Him when He comes again (Matthew
16:27). Till then, the moment of death is Satan's
final opportunity to attack the true believer; but
God has sent His angels to guard us at that time.

In telling the story in Luke 16 Jesus says that
the beggar was "carried by the angels." He was
not only escorted; he was carried. What an experience that must have been for Lazarus! He had
lain begging at the gate of the rich man until his
death, but then suddenly he found himself carried
by the mighty angels of God!

Once I stood in London to watch Queen Elizabeth return from an overseas trip. I saw the parade
of dignitaries, the marching bands, the crack
troops, the waving flags. I saw all the splendor
that accompanies the homecoming of a queen.
However, that was nothing compared to the homecoming of a true believer who has said good-by
here to all of the suffering of this life and been
immediately surrounded by angels who carry him

164

upward to the glorious welcome awaiting the redeemed in heaven.

The Christian should never consider death a tragedy. Rather he should see it as angels do: They realize that joy should mark the journey from time to eternity. The way to life is by the valley of death, but the road is marked with victory all the way. Angels revel in the power of the resurrection of Jesus, which assures us of our resurrection and guarantees us a safe passage to heaven.

Hundreds of accounts record the heavenly escort of angels at death. When my maternal grandmother died, for instance, the room seemed to fill with a heavenly light. She sat up in bed and almost laughingly said, "I see Jesus. He has His arms outstretched toward me. I see Ben [her husband who had died some years earlier] and I see the angels." She slumped over, absent from the body but present with the Lord.

When I was a student in a Bible school a godly young missionary volunteer was suddenly taken ill. The physician said she had only a few hours to live. Her young husband and one or two faculty members were in the room when she suddenly exclaimed, "I see Jesus. I can hear the singing of the angels."

The Reverend A. A. Talbot, missionary to China, was at the bedside of a dying Chinese Christian. Suddenly the room was filled with heavenly music. The Chinese Christian looked up with a radiant smile exclaiming, "I see Jesus standing at the right hand of God, and Margaret Gay is with Him." (Margaret Gay was the Talbots' little daughter who had died months before.)

Dying patients are given so many drugs today that we do not hear as many of these stories now. But to those who face death in Christ it is a glorious experience. The Bible guarantees every believer an escorted journey into the presence of Christ by the holy angels.

The angelic emissaries of the Lord are often sent not only to catch away the redeemed of the Lord at death, but also to give hope and joy to those who remain, and to sustain them in their loss. He has promised to give "the oil of joy for mourning, the garment expressive of praise instead of a heavy, burdened and failing spirit. . . ." (Isaiah 61:3 Amp.B.).

Today man has been overtaken by an increasing sense of gloom about life. In his *Responding to Suicidal Crisis*, Doman Lum quotes Minna Field on the inadequacy of the counsel and treatment given by those who merely "attempt to escape what is to them an unbearable prospect by a pat on the back and by telling the patient that he is talking nonsense." Death seminars are now being held in major medical centers, and teams of psychiatrists, psychologists and therapists are constantly encouraged to become involved. Robert J. Lifton, in studying the cessation of life, points out in the same book some interesting views held by survivors of the atomic destruction of Hiroshima.

He says that "There was a lasting sense of an overwhelming and permanent encounter with death. As a result, there was a breakdown of faith or trust in any human structure, a psychological closure in which people literally numbed themselves to any emotional feelings regarding death, and an overwhelming sense of guilt and self-condemnation as if they were responsible for the tragedy. . . . We are obsessed with the fear of sudden death . . . and recognize the unpredictable nature of life."

In popular thinking you and I have heard people speaking of death as "crossing the Jordan." It is found in spirituals and in some hymns of the Christian faith. It comes, of course, from the victorious march of the Israelites who crossed the Jordan to enter the Promised Land. They passed over Jordan on dry ground. By analogy we can consider that the ministering angels will see us safely across the Jordan River of death as we enter the promised land of heaven. So the Christian does not sorrow as those who have no hope (I Thessalonians 4:13). When the Apostle Paul spoke of his own approaching death, he said, "We are confident, I say, and willing rather to be absent from the body, and to be present with the Lord" (II Corinthians 5:8). When that glorious physical and spiritual separation takes place, the angels will be there to escort us into the presence of our Savior with abounding joy, and it will mean "life everlasting."

The Wonderful Welcome to Come

I believe that death can be beautiful. I have come to look forward to it, to anticipate it with joy and expectation. I have stood at the side of many people who died with expressions of triumph on their faces. No wonder the Bible says, "Precious in the sight of the Lord is the death of His saints" (Psalm 116:15). No wonder David said, "Yea, though I walk through the valley of the shadow of death, I will fear no evil" (Psalm 23:4).

You may be filled with dread at the thought of death. Just remember that at one moment you may be suffering, but in another moment, you will be instantly transformed into the glorious likeness of our Savior. The wonders, beauties, splendor and grandeur of heaven will be yours. You wil be surrounded by these heavenly messengers sent by God to bring you home where you may rest from your labors, though the honor of your works will follow you (Revelation 14:13).

No wonder the Apostle Paul said, "Therefore, my beloved brethren, be ye stedfast, unmoveable, always abounding in the work of the Lord, forasmuch as ye know that your labour is not in vain in the Lord" (I Corinthians 15:58).

Are you ready to face life? Are you ready to face death? No one is truly ready to die who has not learned to live for the glory of God. You can put your confidence in Jesus because He died for you, and in that last moment—the greatest crisis of all—He will have His angels gather you in their arms to carry you gloriously, wonderfully into heaven.

CHAPTER 14

Angel Spectators

How would you live if you knew that you were being watched all the time, not only by your parents, wife, husband or children, but by the heavenly host? The Bible teaches in I Corinthians 4:9 that angels are watching us. Paul says we are a "spectacle" to them. A. S. Joppie points out that the word referred to the arenas where first-century crowds went to see animals killed for sport, men battle to the death and, later, Christians torn apart by lions. In using the word spectacle, Paul is picturing this world as one vast arena. All true Christians participate in this great drama as they seek to obey Christ since this throws them into severe conflict with the forces of evil, who are bent on humiliating them. Yet Scripture says, "They did not hold their lives too dear to lay them down" (Revelation 12:11 NEB).

During this conflict, which was not limited to the arena, the angels were watching them, longing to hasten to their rescue to set free those men and women who often went joyfully to their death. Yet God forbade the angels to rush in as armies of deliverance. Nor had He allowed them to rescue Jesus at the cross when He tasted the death of separation from God the Father. The angel spectators were poised and ready to intervene; the attack order never came. Why? Because God's moment of final victory over the vicious forces of evil had not yet come.

As I mentioned earlier we face many perplexing questions today, such as: Why does God permit evil? Why doesn't God intervene and punish sin? Why does God allow disease? Why does God permit catastrophe? Yet God's timing is precise! Angel hosts who witness everything that transpires in our world are not free to bear up the righteous and deliver the oppressed until God gives the signal. One day He will. Christ has reminded us that the wheat and the tares, the righteous and the unrighteous, are to grow in the field together until the harvest time when the holy angels gather God's elect and bring them into His kingdom.

Angels at Attention

As God's angels have watched the drama of this age unfolding they have seen the Christian church established and expand around the world. They miss nothing as they watch the movements of time, "To the intent that now until the principalities and powers in heavenly places might be known by the church the manifold wisdom of God" (Ephesians 3:10). Dr. Joppie reminds us that the word "now" actually covers the vast expanse of this Church age. Angel hosts have witnessed the formation of the Church of Christ Jesus, and have watched the walk of each believer as the Lord worked His grace, love and power into each life. The angels are observing firsthand the building of the body of the true Church in all places of His dominion this very hour.

But what are they thinking as we live in the world's arena? Do they observe us as we stand fast in the faith and walk in righteousness? Or may they be wondering at our lack of commitment? These two possibilities seem evident from Ephesians 3:10: "(The purpose is) that through the church the complicated, many-sided wisdom of God in all its infinite variety and innumerable aspects might now be made known to the angelic rulers and authorities (principalities and powers) in the heavenly sphere" (Amp.B.).

Our certainty that angels right now witness how we are walking through life should mightily influence the decisions we make. God is watching, and His angels are interested spectators too. The Amplified Bible expresses I Corinthians 4:9 this way: "God has made an exhibit of us . . . a show in the world's amphitheatre—with both men and angels (as spectators)." We know they are watching, but in the heat of the battle, I have thought how wonderful it would be if we could hear them cheering.

Incentives for Righteousness

The charge to live righteously in this present world sobers us when we realize that the walk and warfare of Christians is the primary concern of heaven and its angelic hosts. Paul said, "I solemnly charge you in the presence of God and of Christ Jesus and of the chosen angels, that you guard and keep (these rules) . . ." (I Timothy 5:21 Amp.B.). Paul was stirring up Timothy to remember that the elect angels were constantly watching how he served the Savior and lived the Christian life. What fact could provide a greater motivation to righteous living than that? I must say to myself, "Careful, angels are watching!"

It must give the angels great satisfaction to watch the Church of Jesus Christ minister the unsearchable riches of Christ to lost men everywhere. If the angels rejoice over one sinner who repents (Luke 15:10), then the angel hosts are numbered among the spectators in the heavenly grandstands. They are included among those who are referred to as "so great a cloud of witnesses" (Hebrews 12:1); and they never miss any of the details of our earthly pilgrimage. Yet they do not jeer as did the Greek crowds of Paul's day. Rather as we declare the gospel and see our friends saved, they rejoice with us.

In his book, *Though I Walk Through the Valley*, Dr. Vance Havner tells of an old preacher who worked into the night on a sermon for his small congregation. His wife inquired why he spent so much time on a message that he would give to so few. To this the minister replied, "You forget, my dear, how large my audience will be!" Dr. Havner adds that "Nothing is trivial here if heaven looks on. We shall play a better game if, 'seeing we are encompassed,' we remember who is in the grandstand!"

Our valleys may be filled with foes and tears; but we can lift our eyes to the hills to see God and the angels, heaven's spectators, who support us according to God's infinite wisdom as they prepare our welcome home.

CHAPTER 15

Angels in Our Lives Today

In the early days of World War II, Britain's air force saved it from invasion and defeat. In her book, *Tell No Man,* Adela Rogers St. John describes a strange aspect of that weeks-long air war. Her information comes from a celebration held some months after the war, honoring Air Chief Marshall Lord Hugh Dowding. The King, the Prime Minister and scores of dignitaries were there. In his remarks, the Air Chief Marshall recounted the story of his legendary conflict where his pitifully small complement of men rarely slept, and their planes never stopped flying. He told about airmen on a mission who, having been hit, were either incapacitated or dead. Yet their planes kept flying and fighting; in fact, on occasion pilots in other planes would see a figure still operating the controls. What was the explanation? The Air Chief Marshall said he believed angels had actually flown some of the planes whose pilots sat dead at their cockpits.

That angels piloted planes for dead men in the battle for Britain we cannot finally prove. But we have already seen from Scripture some of the things angels have certainly done, can do, and are yet going to do as history approaches its climax. The important question for each of us is how angels can assist *us* in our lives here and now: How do they help us attain victory over the forces of evil? What is our continuing relationship to them?

We know that God has given His angels charge over us so that without their help we could never get the victory over Satan. The Apostle Paul said, "For we wrestle not against flesh and blood, but against principalities, against powers, against the rulers of the darkness of this world, against spiritual wickedness in high places" (Ephesians 6:12). Let's consider how we can gain help from God through angels.

The God of This Age

Lucifer, our archenemy, controls one of the most powerful and well-oiled war machines in the universe. He controls principalities, powers and dominions. Every nation, city, village and individual has felt the hot breath of his evil power. He is already gathering the nations of the world for the last great battle in the war against

Christ—Armageddon. Yet Jesus assures us that Satan is already a defeated foe (John 12:31, 16:11). In II Timothy 1:10 Paul says that Jesus Christ has abolished death and brought life and immortality to light through the gospel. Peter declares that Jesus "has gone into heaven, and is at the right hand of God, with angels, authorities, and powers subject to him" (I Peter 3:22 RSV).

The Defeat of Satan

While Satan is a defeated foe in principle, obviously God has not yet eliminated him from the world scene. The Bible teaches, however, that God will use angels to judge and totally eliminate him from the universe. In Revelation 12 we read of Satan's earlier defeat: "Michael and his angels fought against the dragon; and the dragon fought and his angels, And prevailed not; neither was their place found any more in heaven. And the great dragon was cast out, that old serpent, called the Devil, and Satan, which deceiveth the whole world: he was cast out into the earth, . . ." (verses 7–9). In chapter 20 John describes how Satan's present earthly rule will be temporarily restricted: "And I saw an angel come down from heaven, having the key of the bottomless pit and a great chain in his hand. And he laid hold on the dragon, that old serpent, which is the Devil, and Satan, and bound him a thousand years, And cast him into the bottomless pit, and shut him up, and set a seal upon him, that he should deceive the nations no more, . . ." John then tells us that after a temporary release followed by the last great battle, God will cast Satan into the lake of fire and brimstone, there to be tormented for ever (Revelation 20:10).

Some will say, "It is well and good to talk about the final defeat of the devil but until that happens it doesn't help me because I have to contend with him every day." But this is not the whole story. We have been given specific instructions in Scripture about how to get victory over the devil.

We are told, for example, "Give no opportunity to the devil" (Ephesians 4:27 RSV). In other words, don't leave any vacant places in your heart for him. The Apostle Peter taught, "Be sober, be vigilant; because your adversary the devil, as a roaring lion, walketh about, seeking whom he may devour" (I Peter 5:8). Thus, we cannot be too careful. This includes the injunction to join God's resistance movement: "Whom resist stedfast in the faith" (I Peter 5:9). And James says "Resist the devil, and he will flee from you" (James 4:7).

But these admonitions to be vigilant and to resist tell only part of the story. In addition we can count on the powerful presence of angels many times more numerous and powerful than Satan and his demons. As Increase Mather wrote centuries ago in *Angelographia*, "Angels both good and bad have a greater influence on this world than men are generally aware of. We ought to ad-

mire the grace of God toward us sinful creatures
in that He hath appointed His holy angels to
guard us against the mischiefs of wicked spirits
who are always intending our hurt both to our
bodies and to our souls."

We have already considered Elisha at Dothan,
ringed by apparently overwhelming enemy forces.
Yet if we, like his servant, had open spiritual eyes,
we would see not only a world filled with evil
spirits and powers—but also powerful angels with
drawn swords, set for our defense.

At Dothan thousands of soldiers surrounded the
city and intended to do Elisha harm. Yet he had
peace. His servant, however, did not, and needed
his eyes opened. We, who are troubled, confused,
fearful, frustrated Christians need God to open our
eyes this very moment. As Vance Havner says,
"Our primary problem is not light, but sight. Light
is of no value to a blind man. Reading books
galore on the subject will not reveal the angels
unless our eyes are touched by faith."

We must not get so busy counting demons that
we forget the holy angels. Certainly we are up
against a gigantic war machine. But we are encompassed by a heavenly host so powerful that
we need not fear the warfare—the battle is the
Lord's. We can boldly face Satan and his legions
with all the confidence of the old captain who,
when told that his outfit was completely surrounded, shouted, "Good, don't let any of them
escape." If your valley is full of foes, raise your

sights to the hills and see the holy angels of God arrayed for battle on your behalf.

When Abraham sent his eldest servant back to his blood relations to look for a bride for Isaac he urged him to go confidently because of God's angel: "he shall send his angel before thee, . . . and prosper thy way" (Genesis 24:7,40). Isaiah the prophet said, "In all their affliction he [the Lord] was afflicted, and the angel of his presence saved them" (63:9). God promised Moses in the midst of all his exasperations, "Mine Angel shall go before thee" (Exodus 23:23). The Bible also says we may see the angels God has sent, but fail to recognize them: "Be not forgetful to entertain strangers: for thereby some have entertained angels unawares" (Hebrews 13:2). Angels, whether noticed by men or not, are active in our twentieth-century world too. Are we aware of them?

It was a tragic night in a Chinese city. Bandits had surrounded the mission compound sheltering hundreds of women and children. On the previous night the missionary, Miss Monsen, had been put to bed with a bad attack of malaria, and now the tempter harassed her with questions: "What will you do when the looters come here? When firing begins on this compound, what about those promises you have been trusting?" In his book, *1,000 New Illustrations* (Zondervan, 1960), Al Bryant records the result. Miss Monsen prayed, "Lord, I have been teaching these young people all these years that thy promises are true, and if they fail now, my mouth shall be forever closed; I must go home."

Throughout the next night she was up, ministering to frightened refugees, encouraging them to pray and to trust God to deliver them. Though fearful things happened all around, the bandits left the mission compound untouched.

In the morning, people from three different neighborhood families asked Miss Monsen, "Who were those four people, three sitting and one standing, quietly watching from the top of your house all night long?" When she told them that no one had been on the housetop, they refused to believe her, saying, "We saw them with our own eyes!" She then told them that God still sent angels to guard his children in their hour of danger.

We have also noted the provision of angels. On occasion they have even given food, as we know from the life of Elijah, following his triumph over the priests of Baal. Fearful, tired and discouraged, "As he lay and slept under a juniper tree, behold, then an angel touched him, and said . . . Arise and eat" (I Kings 19:5-7). God has promised, "Are they not all ministering spirits, sent forth to minister for them who shall be heirs of salvation?" (Hebrews 1:14.) Need we think this provisioning by angels ceased thousands of years ago?

When I was visiting the American troops during the Korean War, I was told of a small group of American marines in the First Division who had been trapped up north. With the thermometer at twenty degrees below zero, they were close to freezing to death. And they had had nothing to eat for six days. Surrender to the Chinese seemed their only hope of survival. But one of the men, a Christian, pointed out certain verses of Scripture, and taught his comrades to sing a song of praise to God. Following this they heard a crashing noise, and turned to see a wild boar rushing toward them. As they tried to jump out of his way, he suddenly stopped in his tracks. One of the soldiers raised his rifle to shoot, but before he could fire, the boar inexplicably toppled over. They rushed up to kill him only to find that he was already dead. That night they feasted on meat, and began to regain their strength.

The next morning just as the sun was rising they heard another noise. Their fear that a Chinese patrol had discovered them suddenly vanished as they found themselves face to face with a South Korean who could speak English. He said, "I will show you out." He led them through the forest and mountains to safety behind their own lines. When they looked up to thank him, they found he had disappeared.

Angels in Judgment

As we continue to study how to gain the help of angels in our lives today, we need to look soberly once again at the relation of angels to judgment.

Just before fire and brimstone fell on Sodom

because of its sins, the angel said, "For we will destroy this place . . . the Lord hath sent us to destroy it" (Genesis 19:13).

In Daniel 7:10 the Word of God says, "A fiery stream issued and came forth from before him . . . the judgment was set, and the books were opened." In scores of places in the Bible God tells us that He will use angels to execute His judgments on all those who have refused to obey His will by failing to receive Christ as Savior and Lord. As Jesus said, "The Son of man shall send forth his angels, and they shall gather out of his kingdom all things that offend, and them which do iniquity; and shall cast them into a furnace of fire: there shall be wailing and gnashing of teeth" (Matthew 13:41, 42). Jesus also said, "It shall be more tolerable for Tyre and Sidon at the day of judgment, than for you" (Matthew 11.22). And again, "every idle word that men shall speak, they shall give account thereof in the day of judgment" (Matthew 12:36). "For there is nothing covered, that shall not be revealed; neither hid, that shall not be known" (Luke 12:2).

God is recording not only the words and actions but all the thoughts and intents of our hearts. Someday you and I will have to give an account, and at that time our final destiny will be determined by whether we have received or rejected Jesus. Paul said that God would give "to you who are troubled rest with us, when the Lord Jesus shall be revealed from heaven with his mighty angels, in flaming fire taking vengeance on them that know not God and that obey not the gospel of our Lord Jesus Christ" (II Thessalonians 1:7–8).

Justice demands that the books of life be balanced, but without a final judgment this would be impossible. Laws too are meaningless unless accompanied by a penalty for those who break them. Reason alone should tell us that there must come a time when God will call upon the Hitlers, the Eichmanns and the Stalins of the world for an accounting. Otherwise there is no justice in the universe.

Thousands of wicked men have lived' evil lives and perpetrated their evil designs upon others without seeming to pay any penalty for their misdeeds in this life. However, the Bible says that a time will come when the crooked places will be made straight (Isaiah 45:2). In the great day of God's judgment men will call on Him for mercy, but it will be too late. In that day if men were to seek God, they would not be able to find Him. It would be too late. They could cry out for angels to deliver them, but it would be of no avail.

Angels Rejoice in the Salvation of Sinners

While angels will play an important role in executing the judgment of God on those who refuse Jesus Christ as Savior and Lord, yet at the same time the Bible informs us that they also rejoice in the salvation of sinners. Jesus tells several striking stories in Luke 15. In the first, a man had a hundred sheep. When one was lost, he left the ninety-nine in the wilderness to seek him. When he found the sheep he slung it over his own shoulders and brought it back to the fold. At home he summoned all his friends, saying, "Rejoice with me: for I have found my sheep which was lost" (verse 6). Jesus said, "I say unto you, that likewise joy shall be in heaven over one sinner that repenteth, more than over ninety and nine just persons, which need no repentance" (verse 7).

His second story is that of a woman who lost a valuable silver coin. She looked everywhere. She swept her house carefully. At last when she recovered the coin she called all her friends and neighbors saying, "Rejoice with me; for I have found the piece which I had lost" (verse 9). "Likewise, I say unto you, there is joy in the presence of the angels of God over one sinner that repenteth" (Luke 15:10).

In these two parables is not Jesus telling us that the angels of heaven have their eyes on every person? They know the spiritual condition of everybody on the face of the earth. Not only does God love you, but the angels love you too. They are anxious for you to repent and turn to Christ for salvation before it is too late. They know the terrible dangers of hell that lie ahead. They want you to turn toward heaven, but they know that this is a decision that you and you alone will have to make.

A rich young ruler came running to kneel before Christ one day, and asked, "Good Master, what shall I do that I may inherit eternal life?" (Mark 10:17). When Peter had preached his great sermon at Pentecost, Luke says the people were "pricked in their heart, and said unto Peter, . . . what shall we do?" (Acts 2:37). The African nobleman riding in the chariot across the desert talked with Philip the evangelist. Suddenly the nobleman stopped his chariot and said, "What doth hinder me?" (Acts 8:36). At midnight the Philippian jailer asked Paul and Silas, "Sirs, what must I do to be saved?" (Acts 16:30). Modern man forever asks this same question. It is old, but always new. It is just as relevant today as it was in the past.

Just what must you do to cause the angels to rejoice? How do you become reconciled to God? How do you repent of your sin? A simple question demands a simple answer. Jesus made everything so simple, and we have made it so complicated. He spoke to people in short sentences, using everyday words, illustrating His message with never-to-be-forgotten stories. He presented the message of God in such simplicity that many were amazed at what they heard. They could hardly believe their ears, because the message was so simple.

In the Acts of the Apostles, the Philippian jailer asked the Apostle Paul, "What must I do to be saved?" Paul gave him a very simple answer, "Believe on the Lord Jesus Christ, and thou shalt be saved" (Acts 16:30, 31). This is so simple that

186

millions stumble over it. The one and only way you can be converted is to believe on the Lord Jesus Christ as your own personal Lord and Savior. You don't have to straighten out your life first. You don't have to try to give up some habit that is keeping you from God. You have tried all that and failed many times. You can come "just as you are." The blind man came just as he was. The leper came just as he was. The thief on the cross came just as he was. You can come to Christ right now wherever you are and just as you are— and the angels of heaven will rejoice!

Some of the greatest and most precious words recorded in all of Scripture were spoken by Satan himself (not that he intended it to be so). In his discussion with God about Job, he said, "Hast not thou made an hedge about him, and about his house, and about all that he hath on every side? thou hast blessed the work of his hands, and his substance is increased in the land" (Job 1:10).

As I look back over my life I remember the moment I came to Jesus Christ as Savior and Lord. The angels rejoiced! Since then I have been in thousands of battles with Satan and his demons. As I yielded my will and committed myself totally to Christ—as I prayed and believed—I am convinced that God "put a hedge about me," a hedge of angels to protect me.

The Scripture says there is a time to be born and a time to die. And when my time to die comes an angel will be there to comfort me. He will give me peace and joy even at that most critical hour, and usher me into the presence of God, and I will dwell with the Lord forever. Thank God for the ministry of His blessed angels!